"Toni's direct, passionate voice urges us gently, relentlessly, toward this ... here ... now ... and away from the crowded fantasy of 'me.'"

—LENORE FRIEDMAN, author of
Meetings with Remarkable Women

"In the subtlest religious teachings the practice is to 'listen.' But it is usually not enough for us. We want something to do. Toni listens and invites us to do the same. The reader feels as though he or she is being spoken to directly."

—ARTHUR BRAVERMAN, author of
A Quiet Room: The Poetry of Zen Master Jakushitsu

"Toni Packer has a mind swift and clear as sandpipers scurrying on a beach in sunlight. She invites us again and again to wake up to this moment!"

—SANDY BOUCHER, author of
Hidden Spring: A Buddhist Woman Confronts Cancer

"'One comes to retreat,' Toni says, for 'some freeing from the self-centered cocoon that separates us.' If you come to this book for the same reason, you will not be disappointed. Toni reminds us that we are all part of 'one vibrant aliveness,' and she manages to do so with mischievousness and a compassionate acknowledgment of our suffering."

—SUSAN MOON, author of *The Life and Letters of Tofu Roshi*, and editor of *Turning Wheel*

The Wonder of Presence

AND THE WAY
OF MEDITATIVE INQUIRY

TONI PACKER

FOREWORD BY
Michael Atkinson

SHAMBHALA
Boston & London
2002

Shambhala Publications, Inc.
Horticultural Hall
300 Massachusetts Avenue
Boston, Massachusetts 02115
www.shambhala.com

9 8 7 6 5 4 3 2 1

First Edition
Printed in the United States of America

∞ This edition is printed on acid-free paper that meets the
American National Standards Institute z39.48 Standard.
Distributed in the United States by Random House, Inc.,
and in Canada by Random House of Canada Ltd

LIBRARY OF CONGRESS CATALOGING-IN-PUBLICATION DATA

Packer, Toni, 1927–
The wonder of presence / Toni Packer.—1st ed.
p.   cm.
ISBN 1-57062-875-0 (alk. paper)
1. Spiritual life.   2. Spiritual life—Zen Buddhism.   I. Title.
BL624 .P33   2002
291.4'4—dc21   2001049805

To Kyle

Contents

PART THREE

Relationship

PART FOUR

Conditioning and Wholeness

Foreword

*T*HE RAIN CAME DOWN in sheets—gallons, not drops—and I looked for a place to dive for cover. Monsoon season was technically over, but the skies opened suddenly and quite completely that afternoon in Thailand in the early 1990s. From the doorway of his *kuti,* an orange-robed monk waved me his way, and I ran for the shelter he offered. On a long trip through Asia, I had taken a vacation from the vacation to meditate for a week at this genial and friendly *wat* in northern Thailand. No formal program was under way, but there was room for me to sit by myself each day in a thatch-roofed platform that overlooked a pond and a tangle of trees and vines, where I would neither disturb nor be disturbed by much coming or going. The rain had caught me far from my thatched roof, though, and the arm and smile that beckoned me to shelter belonged to an older monk, a German national who had years ago taken refuge in this forest, this temple, these orange robes. His *kuti* was dry, his hospitality complete, and his English good. As the river of rain continued just inches from where we sat, we fell into talk.

"America," he said. "If you come from America, you have the chance to study with one of the truly great spiritual teachers." Odd, I thought, coming from one who had left the West and had dwelt for decades in the heartland of traditional Buddhist teaching. And who would that be? "Toni Packer," he said to my astonishment and pleasure. I had, at the time, been working with Toni for several years. "She works so freely. No need for all this," he said with a sweep of the hand that seemed to include the monastery's great Buddha statues and dharma hall and the sound of monks chanting, just audible over the roar of the rain. "But," he continued with a smile, even a wink, "one can find what she teaches, even here."

Much has been made of Toni Packer's leaving behind the forms and institutions of traditional Buddhism, of all traditions. Drawn to study Zen, she was lucky enough to find the Rochester Zen Center, in upstate New York, within driving distance of her home. For years she studied there with Roshi Philip Kapleau (whose *Three Pillars of Zen* introduced so many people to practice). Eventually she was named his dharma heir and was expected to assume the central teaching responsibility for the Rochester Zen Center. But even as she rose to this prominence, Toni had begun to doubt the efficacy of the forms which had grown up around the unnamable. Seeing the destructive effects of reliance on tradition in any spiritual tradition, she had been drawn to the work of Krishnamurti, whom she read avidly and went to hear speak near the end of his life. In the end, Toni could not perpetuate the traditions in which she was being elevated. She left behind the center and the credentials it bestowed to work in a way that really did question everything. About half the members of the Rochester Zen Center followed, and in not too long a time, a center where this practice could go forward was built near the (happily named) village of Springwater, New York, some fifty miles south of Rochester. At first called the Genesee Valley Zen Center, it eventually became Springwater Center for Meditative Inquiry and Retreats.

In the early days, the departure may have fostered a sense of high drama and division in the spiritual community. But now, students from Rochester are often found sitting at Springwater; Toni makes visits to an ailing Kapleau Roshi, who has also visited Springwater; many who call themselves Buddhists, as well as many who reject that label, call Springwater their spiritual home; and the old German monk in Thailand can practice the free and open style of meditative inquiry that Toni fosters, "even there" in the heart of a traditional monastery.

Although Toni travels to teach in both Western and Eastern Europe and holds retreats in California, the geographical center from which she moves and to which she returns is Springwater, perched on a hillside in the Finger Lakes region. It is in the retreats conducted there that most who work with her encounter her, and it is from there that most of the talks that form the basis for this book's chapters were given.

Leaving the two-lane highway that leads away from the tiny village of Springwater, a dirt road takes you past a sprinkling of houses, turns into the woods, and winds its way toward the center itself. Fifty yards from a gravel parking lot partly sheltered by the surrounding woodlands, high on the hillside, is a large, modern, wooden building, with great glass windows looking south. Entering a reception area, where racks hold shoes and invite you to leave yours, you find someone from the staff there to greet you. Neatly printed white sheets of paper on a bulletin board give you your room number and your job for the retreat, and you find your way to the room and roommate with whom you will spend the next week, stow away gear, make your bed, and return to the main floor of the building to connect with old friends or to meet new faces, an activity that continues through a serve-yourself dinner of soup and bread at five o'clock. As the conversations continue, most are mindful of the silence that will ensue after the orientation at seven.

The coordinators of the retreat, who are not given any special standing, explain safety procedures and the general mechanics of retreat. Schedules are posted in a number of places, and one is never in doubt about what will be offered next. But here, all activities except work period are optional. You may come to the talks or not, attend sitting periods or go for a walk or take a much needed nap. No credit is given for being on one's cushion early or staying late. And if you need to communicate—and this is the only binding rule other than doing your work assignments—do it with the pencils and pads of paper that are available everywhere throughout the center.

The whole retreat will take place in a silence that is broken only by Toni's talks and in meetings. First the mouth, then (with luck) the mind, may give up the compulsion to chatter. Perhaps in the silence some of that automatic functioning can come into question, can be seen through, even set aside, in the course of a deeper looking.

At first the silence may seem inconvenient, but in time it becomes the solid and flexible basis of the retreat experience. As the interactions that habitually confirm our self-images drop away, the ease and simplicity of moving through the day quietly gives a hint that life might be more like this all the time—not with total silence, certainly, but without that foam of language that forms on what could be the clear water of our actions. When words are exchanged, they could count for something, could be heard as well as spoken.

In the meditation hall that first night, we settle onto our cushions or chairs and enter what Toni has called the work of this moment, being aware of all that is going on within and around us—the sound of the wind, the touch of air currents within the room, the coming and going of our own breathing, and of our thoughts and impulses—just being fully present to whatever arises.

Toni is notorious in the spiritual community for her refusal to instruct people in techniques of meditation. Individuals attending the retreat may count their breaths or recite a mantra to themselves, but that is strictly their own doing (and in no way forbidden or even discouraged, really). Eventually, one comes to the point of trying the simple "awareing" that Toni speaks of so often and so passionately, allowing the mind free of technique to see, to hear, to be with what is going on. Others may call this a version of *shikan taza*, or *maha ati*, or *dzogchen*, but Toni declines to align this clear seeing with any tradition or technique—in fact, she seeks to free it from all traditional assumptions, inviting us to just see, just listen, not with the eyes or ears only but with all our being.

A small bell sounds, and twenty-five minutes of meditation are followed by seven minutes of informal, unstylized walking meditation at a gently ambling pace. Here again, there is complete freedom. Those who want to walk more slowly or quickly, or get some of the tea always supplied in several varieties, or go to the bathroom, or stretch, or leave the meditation area altogether, peel out of and reenter the walking line, which wends its way through the room until that small bell invites those who wish to return to their places and begin sitting again.

So, through several rounds, goes the first evening, ending

with snacks set out in the kitchen for those who want them. Then sleep.

A bell at 5:30 the next morning summons most to wakefulness, and a silent cluster coalesces and dissolves around the various pots of tea waiting, steamy, downstairs in the dining hall. At six, sitting and walking begins again, and after the morning meditation, a hearty breakfast of cooked grains and fruit, followed by a silent work period. In a single hour, virtually all the work that needs to be done at the center is accomplished in silence. Food is chopped, soup made, dishes washed, floors swept, the entire spick-and-span ambiance made even cleaner. And then this silent flurry, which itself becomes quite focusing over time, subsides into an hour in which one can rest, read, or take a walk. At ten the meditation begins again, and after the first round of sitting and walking, it is time for Toni to speak.

Sitting in a place of no special prominence, eyes closed, she names the day, takes a moment of silence, and begins. Her voice is a little deep—as seems to befit this tall, vibrantly alive, white-haired woman in her early seventies—and it is full of passion and wonder, quietly urgent. Often, she speaks first of the land on which we are sitting—the rustle of wind, bird sounds, the faint roar of a plane overhead, the warmth of the sunlight streaming through the many windows, the buzz of flies in summer, drip of rain, the sound of winter's icy branches knocking against one another. The sense of nature's presence is never far from the surface, even as the talk works its way through other concerns. In midsentence Toni may echo the caw of a bird from the nearby woods: no division between reflection and nature, the topic at hand and the great world in which it arises.

The first day's talk almost always centers on listening, which is in a way the start and the finish of Toni's work. Can we come to listening freshly, whether or not we've ever worked in this way before, whether these retreats are a new experience or a way of life for us? Can we listen in such a way that we inquire along with Toni, not listening to her as an authority, but letting her listening awaken our own? Are we agreeing, going along hoping for the best, looking for a secret, willing to accept things doubtful in order to achieve some special state? Or are we genuinely asking, sentence by sentence, "How is it with me? Is this true of me? How am I responding at this moment?" Can we attend not only to what the mind hears but also to the hearing itself, and to how the whole bodymind responds throughout its network of nerves and muscles, ideas and memories? Can we truly listen?

When Toni speaks, the language she uses is the stuff of ordinary English, but one begins to notice little alterations here and there—how infrequently the personal pronouns get used, how "aware" has metamorphosed from adjective to verb, as when Toni speaks of awaring the moment in all its richness, and that awaring is seen as more primary than the individual in whom it is happening. Such language is not a repeating machine but a vehicle for discovery.

Silences often punctuate the talks, and after a time there comes a silence followed by the words, "We will end here for today." But it is only the talk that is ended. The listening goes forward into the rich silence of the day's unfolding. More sitting and walking, lunch of soup and bread and fruit, abundant, a walk across the meadows or through the woodland paths that surround the center, a pause to sit and listen to the waters of the cascade or watch the clouds reflected in the pond's surface, now wind wrinkled, now clear. A chance to exercise and then return to the sitting room for more sitting quietly, doing nothing. Dinner, another walk perhaps, and as the angled light of sunset gives way to twilight, then darkness, the evening's rhythm of sitting and walking is again under way in the meditation hall.

As the day unfolds, there are regular opportunities to meet with Toni in small groups or individually. Once or twice a day, half a dozen or so people gather in the meeting room to see what emerges and wants to be looked at, questions arising out of the shared silence. In these meetings you may find yourself hearing, and being heard, with an extraordinary openness that brings genuine freshness and transparency to what had seemed stale and intractable.

Or you may choose to meet with Toni individually. You come when you need to, when a question is ripe, perhaps, or when a difficulty seems insoluble, a matter urgent. Entering the interview room, you find Toni ready to receive whatever you bring—a problem with sitting, the breakup of a relationship, a new discovery, a recurring anger, a sudden opening. She is there to look into it deeply with you. Everything is accepted, everything workable, including, most completely, yourself—you who enter this room, hesitant or anxious, calm or full of joy or confusion. If you want simply to listen together to the play of wind and the sound of breathing, it is enough. For in that listening is the very openness we can bring to our problems, our relationships, our discoveries, our lives, moment by moment. The awareness heightened, the situation explored freshly, one leaves the meeting with a smile, perhaps a hug, to return to chair or cushion and look again silently into the matter.

There is no drive to produce an enlightenment experience, no attempt to produce any experience at all, but instead a cultivation of deep listening, deep looking into the situations in which we find ourselves, and into the very quality of looking and listening. For the very act of looking openly without preconception, without boundary, is itself an expression of the awakened mind. And this clarity is there to be found, not once and for all in some definitive crossing of a boundary, but "for moments at a time," as Toni likes to say.

Neither long nor short, those moments are not to be measured in time. The grip of time itself seems to loosen as we settle into listening openly, into seeing without knowing, as one of Toni's early book titles put it. The silence becomes vibrant—itself a kind of listening—no longer a background. And the emergence from it of bird sound and plane hum, of the crunch of gravel underfoot and of the grain of Toni's voice, only seem to affirm that sound and silence are one in this listening, are facets of one presence, as are those in whom the listening takes place.

On the last day, instead of speaking in her own words, Toni reads—typically from the writing of Zen master Huang Po, from Krishnamurti, from the poet Mary Oliver and others, not claiming some traditional sanction but exploring the reverberations of listening in the minds and writings of others. Retreatants too begin to shift gears, as they turn back toward the world of speech and interaction that awaits them at retreat's end. What can be taken from retreat back into daily life? The alertness of listening? The openness of a mind that is not always racing—or an openness *to* that mind? Since none of these is actually "produced," none can be carried forward or left behind. But for almost everyone something shifts, and we leave more awake, a little wiser, knowing less than when we came.

The listening that emerges while sitting quietly doing nothing is not confined to retreats. It is possible in the midst of a city as well as on a rural hillside, and it is certainly possible while reading this book. The talks gathered in these pages speak from and of that spaciousness, which can be found in our daily living. Reading and hearing these words, we can listen openly, inquire deeply, each step of the way asking, "How is it with me?" For it is our very nature, the most fundamental level of our being, that speaks and that listens here.

—Michael Atkinson
University of Cincinnati

Preface

AS IN MY PREVIOUS BOOKS, *The Work of This Moment* (Boston: Shambhala Publications, Inc., 1990; Boston: Charles E. Tuttle Co., Inc., 1995) and *The Light of Discovery* (Boston: Charles E. Tuttle Co., Inc., 1995), this volume of writings is a heartfelt response to many readers' requests for covering new topics that have come up in talks since the earlier publications. People engaged in meditative inquiry find it helpful not only to hear talks and listen to tapes but also to be able to open a book and read the written word at their own pace and rhythm.

The single most significant question for every one of us remains: "Can the awareness and loving intelligence experienced during retreat at moments of silent presence also operate in our hectic daily lives that are so heavily controlled by unconscious automatic reactions? Is it possible to live from moment to moment with a deepening awareness of our powerful conditioning that keeps us isolated and suffering, not in order to judge, resist, or fight it, but to shed the light of understanding on *what we actually are*—in ignorance as well as in open wisdom and compassion?"

Most of the chapters in *The Wonder of Presence* have their origin in talks given during retreats in Springwater and California. The only exceptions are a piece of correspondence dating back to 1996, a conversation with Lenore Friedman previously published in her book *Being Bodies* (Boston: Shambhala Publications, Inc., 1997), and a dialogue that took place at the Buddhism in America Conference in Boston in 1997. Every chapter has been freshly looked at, and most of them I have revised so much that they may bear only a faint resemblance to their originals. It is the amazing nature of deeply entering into a fundamental question that the human mind, when open and unpreoccupied, will come upon new insights, expressions, and illustrations that may supersede previous verbal renderings. For those who are interested in dates, most of the chapters originated in talks held in the years 1998 to 2000. Practically all of the rewriting took place in the year 2000.

The words written in this volume may not lend themselves to satisfying our hunger for information about ourselves, even though the mind can superficially use them that way. Rather than just conveying knowledge about ourselves, they invite each one of us to stop in our automatic thinking tracks—to pause, look, and listen freshly this very instant of reacting, wanting, fearing, paining, and pleasuring. In this way the written word may become a guide not only to seeing ourselves in a new light but also to partaking in the amazing stillness of awareness that makes our conditioning transparent and clear *as conditioning*.

The book has been divided into four parts: "What Is Meditative Inquiry?," "Me and You and the World," "Relationship," and "Conditioning and Wholeness." Even though each chapter fits into its specific category, it also fits all of them in that the fundamental question of who and what we truly are, and the wonder of illuminating awareness, permeate them all.

The immense challenge to each one of us is this: Can we live our daily lives, at least for moments at a time, in the wonder of presence that is the creative source of everything?

Acknowledgments

*T*HIS BOOK WOULD not have come into existence without the dedicated help of many dear friends: d. Allen gave most generously of his enthusiasm, time, and energy to select talks and send them out for transcription, as well as to edit the material and organize it meaningfully into four sections. Stew Glick spent a lot of time setting up new computers and configuring them so that I could switch between home and workplace with ease. Susan McCallum was always there when I needed to talk about a problem, helping me get through all kinds of computer enigmas, using her own considerable skills, time, and energy to put the manuscript into its final shape, making suggestions along the way as well as proofreading the end result. Many thanks to Michael Atkinson for giving of his valuable time to write the foreword; to the faithful transcribers of innumerable talks: Laura Abrams, d. Allen, Michael Atkinson, Sandy Gray, Susan McCallum, and Dennis Peak; to Joan Tollifson and Sue Christopherson for helpful suggestions on chapter 6; and to Peter Turner and Emily Bower of Shambhala Publications for happily welcoming the manuscript. Last but not least, my heartfelt gratitude to all the people who keep coming to Springwater to participate in the work of this moment as retreatants, guests, and staff members, and to my beloved late husband, Kyle, who supported me in this unfathomable work into his dying days.

PART ONE

What Is Meditative Inquiry?

1

The Wonder of Presence

WHAT A QUIET SUNDAY IT IS, overflowing with golden light! Taking a walk this morning along the driveway, with the sound of crunching white snow, evergreen branches shedding sprays of glistening crystals when touched by the breeze, the taste of tiny flakes on lips and cheeks, descending to the freezing creek with its gurgling waters splashing over icy rocks playfully sparkling in the light of the sun, crows calling loudly to each other throughout the woods—what heart would not be gladdened?

Under a vast blue sky this wondrous presence is here, replacing habitual worrisome thoughts and feelings. They can't survive the deep silence of open being. It is not brought about by anything or anyone—it is here without effort, without time.

In this sunlit hall with green plants cascading down the wall, sitting together, listening, breathing, and wondering in stillness, we are all alone and yet all one. When thoughts about my problems, my fears, my needs and desires abate in silent presence, what could possibly divide us?

If thoughts are whirling about, let them be like dancing

snowflakes in empty space! This moment of light and warmth and cool air, inhaling and exhaling softly—are we here? This instant of opening eyes and ears widely, beholding the wooden floor, the distant blue hills, and silent people all around, what else is there?

Is the mind thinking about all this, or can it quiet down in simple wondering without knowing?

2

What Is the Meditation Practice at Springwater?

C AN LISTENING AND SPEAKING come out of silence? The silence of breathing, of physical sensations, birds twittering, motors humming . . . Is "being here" utterly simple?

In the midst of listening and chirping, humming and breathing, people want to know, "What meditation practice do you teach here? What should my practice be?" This is a frequent question asked by people interested in meditation, expecting to be taught a practice, wishing to become good at it. But where does the question itself come from? Is there an assumption that meditation must involve a practice? That a teacher is needed who knows what we have to do, what guidance we need, what path to follow, where to go? Is there a deep need to ask someone else, "What should I do? What is the right thing to do here?" Do we feel a need to be reassured in our persistent doubts: "Am I doing it right? Am I doing enough? Am I doing as well as the others?"

Each of us has a different motive for taking up spiritual practice. Yet a motive is there for all of us, isn't there? Maybe we are hearing an implied criticism in that question—that I shouldn't have any motive, because that is wrong. Whatever is being said here, no matter how critical it may sound, can there remain moments of simple listening? This heavily conditioned brain has difficulty in hearing anything innocently. Whatever is heard is fitted into a preexisting context laid down in the past. It hears criticism where there is none intended. It assumes that conditioned reactions that are pointed out in a talk are *wrong* and therefore the opposite—no conditioning—must be right. And that therefore I need to get rid of my conditioning, and please tell me what practice will do that for me. On and on. No criticism is implied, just watching the mind rattling on.

How simple can the listening be? Is it humanly possible to listen without adding interpretations, judgments, conclusions? It all happens at lightning speed. No one is doing it. The brain interprets, judges, concludes, demands answers according to its accumulated structures laid down in the past. The body orchestrates the process with an array of sensations from the most pleasurable to the most painful.

In our daily life there is so much living in brain-made stories and so little waking in plain unadulterated presence. There is constant entanglement in habitual reactions with little awareness. Hearing this, are we judging ourselves negatively for doing that, putting ourselves down? For example, we may routinely imagine being criticized for not making enough effort and therefore think that we need more discipline, more external structure to submit to. We go from teacher to teacher looking for the one who will finally get us enlightened. We are eager to try a new meditation practice, hoping it will be more effective than what we have done before. Tomorrow we may think and feel differently again.

Let's come back to "What is the practice here?" Actually we dropped the word "practice" long ago because it implies doing something repetitively. To become good at singing opera, you have to practice scales endlessly. When you hear this you may say: "No, in my meditation I don't repeat anything—no mantra, no koan, no counting breaths. I just sit and attend, and that is what I call 'my practice.'" That's OK! We can call anything by any name we wish, just as long as we share the same meaning when we communicate with each other.

So, whether we call it a practice or not, can we behold whatever is happening from moment to moment, living it choicelessly? Can we appreciate how difficult that is? Can we intimately watch the way we think, feel, respond—the manner in which we talk and cry to ourselves? The way we react to what we think others think about us, the manner in which we constantly look for love and approval and are afraid of being criticized, and the way we hate the boredom of nothing exciting happening during our sitting?

Let's take that for a moment. We say we are bored or afraid, but can we go beyond the mere label? What is boredom? What is fear? Can we wonder about it more than superficially, not being satisfied with labels? Labels prevent looking. The brain feels comfortable with labels, feels calmer after an explanation and a reason has been given. But an explanation does not ultimately satisfy, because fear, anger, and insecurity cannot be explained away. They are here, beckoning to be looked at directly, to be felt and touched as they trickle into awareness.

Someone asked what I mean by being in touch with fear. Shall we go into this together? What is it actually that we label "fear"? What mental and bodily movements are happening when I say, "I am afraid"? In the light of this question one begins to directly experience physical contractions, tensions, and vibrations that feel highly unpleasant and thoroughly unwanted. We do not want to feel like that one bit and automatically endeavor to get rid of the discomfort. It's a conditioned reflex—trying to get rid of the unpleasant. All the memories of feeling afraid are mobilized. They direct: "Don't go there! It's too dangerous, too unbearable! It'll kill me!" Memory is relentlessly shielding immediate experience with stories from the past. But are they telling the truth? How do I know that this feeling is dangerous, that I can't survive touching it? I truly don't know this. Have I ever touched fear directly, without a hairbreadth of separation? So can there be a pause in the habitual reactions and a wondering instead, *What is this?* Not "knowing" it, but directly experiencing what is ailing this bodymind. It always turns out different from what I thought it was! There is nothing dangerous in being completely, unconditionally what is. The only danger lies in maintaining the defensive cover.

Is there any resistance left to touching fear directly? If so, what is resistance? Can we feel it out? Isn't it a pushing away arising from habitual aversion to being directly in touch? The thought "I don't like this" already embodies a physical bracing against the sensations. It is a palpable tensing of the body against itself. How amazing! The bodymind produces tensions in accordance with past memories and then resists what it just produced! The result is more pain and conflict. This is not just intellectual talk. It is an honest description of what is directly observable in all of us.

In this inward listening, can resistance be clearly felt and seen and abate on its own? It takes subtle attention because we are so used to our resistances that we do not often notice them directly. But as we listen and watch openly, there is less interference from memory telling us what everything is, and how it will be in the future. There is less stuff surrounding and concealing what is actually here. Resistance can become transparent. See it! Feel the body tensing against itself, and wonder whether it has to be that way.

So why do we need a special practice? Isn't there enough going on every instant, ready to be discovered anew in spacious listening and looking? Do we need to focus concentration on anything special? Isn't being here in a new, spacious way all that is needed? And if it feels anything but spacious right now, can we feel the *tightness* of wanting something other than what's here right now?

By "spacious" I mean no effort to exclude anything that's happening right now. Making an effort to concentrate on a particular practice creates the separate "concentrator." Spaciousness is the absence of a meditator having to concentrate on something. It is the absence of *me* or *mine* as a reference point. Have we ever noticed how everything and everyone we perceive is somehow referred to *me?* In some way or other *I* always comes into the picture: how *I* like it, how *I* can use it, what it means to *me*, what *my* advantages and disadvantages are, and so on. The *I* is there, as a thickly enmeshed reference point that cannot listen innocently to what somebody is saying without thinking that maybe they are being critical of *me*, not liking *me*. Maybe *I* did something wrong.

Well, maybe someone is really referring to something I have done wrong. Can that be heard silently without immediate defensiveness, aggression, or paranoia? This may sound idealistic, but we are asking seriously whether it is possible to move through one's day and be with people without referring everything to a personal *me*. It is a good question to ask and a wonderful way of discovering the nature of the *me*. The answer is enfolded in simple moment-to-moment listening.

We were discussing spaciousness, an alive wondering that needs no practice. It needs to *happen*. Hearing these words, do I want it to happen to me because it sounds like the salvation from my mess?

It is not in the words. It is not a practice. It is not subject to will. It is birds singing, air moving gently, story coming and going, breath flowing, back aching, heart beating, sun shining, beholding it all in silence with an open heart that does not go anywhere.

3

Meditative Questioning

SOMEONE ASKED in a group meeting: "You have talked about questioning something without immediately looking for the answer. But I come here in order to find answers to my questions. Don't we all do that?"

Let us first clarify what we mean by questioning. I can see two different ways of questioning. In our normal everyday life we habitually expect to get answers to our questions. At home and in school special attention was given to us when we asked good questions. Most parents and teachers like it when their children ask them for information or for advice. We all love to give answers. Not that we always know what we are talking about—often we say something without having given it much thought at all—any answer seems so much better than not knowing what to say. We have a real urge to be "in the know." Knowing things is highly valued—we are well rewarded for having all kinds of information stored in our brains and being able to pass it on to others. We take it for granted that asking questions means having to get or to give answers—the sooner the better. Drawing a blank or saying "I don't know" is considered weak or embarrassing.

Meditative questioning is different—we come to it after

having exhausted most conventional answers. Something inside remains in doubt, restless, dissatisfied. The questions themselves may vary—they may be about the nature and cause of anger, resistance, resentment, attachment, anxiety, or suffering. Or they may be more fundamental: "What am I?" "What is the meaning of life and death?"

Is it possible to hold a question without immediately searching for answers? It is a different mode of mind: Instead of automatically seeking the relief that a superficial answer provides, can we start with not knowing and ask the question into not knowing? I'm not talking conceptually, even though the brain may already have made a concept out of "not knowing." Not knowing means putting aside what I already know and being curious to observe freshly, openly, what is actually taking place right now in the light of the question. Not knowing means putting up with the discomfort of no immediate answer.

Not knowing about anger means observing the energy movement as it arises, unfolds, and keeps going. Can we abstain from our habitual explanations and watch carefully how anger wells up when someone does something "wrong" (in contrast to what I know is "right"), when someone thwarts my wishes, when I am criticized, or when I don't get what others are getting—"the unfairness of it all," and so on? Watch how the incident translates itself into a story spun out by the brain, and how this story keeps triggering the chemicals that maintain the angry emotions long after the original stimulus has passed. Listen inwardly to the negative judgments about myself for having gotten angry, or to the justifications and rationalizations provided by the brain to keep my image intact. Follow the whole ongoing process with a mind that is open and interested in inquiring and discovering the facts directly.

This kind of questioning is no different from asking "Who or what am I?" The essence of meditative inquiry is not obtaining answers but wondering patiently without knowing. We may have heard spiritual teachers say, "The answer is in the question." I used to hear Krishnamurti say it time and time again but in the beginning didn't understand what he meant. You cannot understand it by trying to figure it out. It has to reveal itself clearly in the questioning itself when it is open and innocent. Awaring without knowing.

Someone asked: "Isn't the 'deepest answer' to our questions the fact of separation? And if so, why don't we work the other way around—from answer to question to see how our problems are expressions of our belief in a separate self?"

The questioner seemed to be asking, "Why don't you clarify the problem of separation at the very beginning?" Let's go into that question together. Actually, we do talk about our true state of being—it cannot be avoided. In truth *there is no separation*. When the sense of self is in abeyance, we are all whole—not just whole but *the whole*, without all the anxiety that inevitably goes with the sense of a separate *me*. In living presence there is no sense of time, no inside or outside, no me or you—just wholesome being without walls that would separate and divide us.

When I said this in the meeting, someone else responded: "But we can't all become Toni Packer! We are just poor schmucks who have to deal with negative emotions like fear and anger."

Does anyone really believe that Toni does *not* have to deal with fear, anger, or sadness? She does! I am intimately acquainted with all the emotions and moods that human beings experience. We are not different from each other—we are schmucks in our conditioned ways and at the same time we lack nothing. Why do we believe that we have to become like someone else in order to awaken to our intrinsic whole-ness? Being here, undivided as we are, is not a matter of becoming—it is so right now, whether we realize it or not.

It is risky to talk about all this as though there were an "answer" before the question is alive. First of all, is it clear that mere words are not the real thing? The best description is only a description, nothing more. The brain is eager to know things, yet it needs direct insight to see that knowledge is not the same as insight. Thinking cannot see its own way of hiding the truth. Thinking does not *see*. Secondly, hearing someone say that we are fundamentally undivided easily creates discontent and even guilt when we feel anything but whole—when we are aching with the fear and pain of separation.

So how do we listen when someone speaks of our funda-mental wholeness? Do we compare ourselves with the speaker and despair of ever being like him or her, do we resist or reject what is being said to protect ourselves, or can we sim-ply listen and wonder with a new innocence?

Years back, reading a quote of Krishnamurti in a book by Alan Watts, and also coming upon a collection by D. T. Suzuki of Zen anecdotes, I couldn't understand at all what they really meant. I couldn't fathom where someone would be coming from to be able to say what they were saying. I couldn't understand it, but neither could I be done with it. When words move us strangely even though we do not grasp them, can we simply hold them patiently in our heart?

Amazingly enough, the moment comes when suddenly they become clear—no longer as words, but as an unshakable truth.

4

A Few Tips for Sitting

THE EYES

During retreat people often feel discouraged about continuously getting absorbed in fantasies and daydreams. Sometimes sitters feel sleepy, droopy, and yet keep their eyes closed. Here is a suggestion if you find yourself battling tiredness, dreaminess or trancelike states: Try keeping your eyes open. Not completely open, not looking to see things, but half-open and half-closed, relaxed, with lowered gaze. In the beginning this may feel uncomfortable and unnatural, because the eyes desperately want to see and know things. Without that energy they easily close and go to sleep. Dreaming is so much easier than staying awake and alert.

I keep my eyes closed during a talk, so don't take that as a model. Having the eyes closed while talking makes it easier to see what I am saying. Also, when the eyes are tired, it feels relaxing to close them and yet remain alert without falling asleep. In most cases, it's good to keep the eyes partly open, letting some light in but not trying to focus on anything. This position of the eyes allows for a quiet yet alert brain.

There is no guarantee that this will happen immediately, but there is a palpable connection.

It took me a quite a while in Zen training until this way of keeping the eyes became effortless and natural. During the first year or longer they were tearing relentlessly—not from sorrow, but from being unaccustomed to any kind of wakeful relaxation. Eyes are programmed to look, scan, and know things. This immediately triggers the brain to interpret what is seen and to react to the interpretation in one way or another. Needless to say, most of these interpretations are inaccurate.

The eyes want to look at people to find out whether they are friend or foe, happy or angry, whether they approve of me, ignore me, or are impressed by me. The beauty of keeping the eyes down in retreat with other people is to discover firsthand how deeply conditioned we are to establishing some kind of "security" through eye contact. If we manage to keep the eyes from roving around for information and remain still, we can find a new kind of inner strength that does not need to look at the eyes of others for approval. And when we do not evaluate others on the basis of our customary eye contact it becomes possible to be in touch with each other in an innocent way. We can also become aware of the prejudices the brain harbors about "other people."

POSTURE

In observing myself I find that I quickly slouch when there is a physical need to relax. Slouching is a far more entrenched habit for me than sitting with a straight back. For a while it feels good to a strained body to slouch, at least until the slouching creates its own aches.

But when I need to listen quietly or inquire deeply with

people in meetings, the back straightens on its own in a natural way. No need to be rigid about proper posture. The back lifts itself up spontaneously as the mind inquires, opens up, and empties out. It is intimately related to our varying states of mind. In experiencing pain, sorrow, anger, fear, or greed, the body manifests each mood in its own ways. In openness and clarity the body feels like no-body.

I found after my husband Kyle's death that there was ceaseless remembering, paining, longing, crying—even a single image of Kyle instantly brought on grief and ache throughout the entire body. But coming here into retreat a couple of weeks later and sitting down quietly in this beautiful spacious hall with many silent people, the body's way of conducting energies changes almost immediately. Sitting quietly there is a natural, effortless gathering of energy away from the mind's habitual networking in memories, with their contractions, pain, and grief. Sitting quietly without expectation or strain, the energy that is normally traveling in the *me-*network now works freely in clearing body and mind. Can we open up to this undivided wholeness that is our quintessence, not in a grasping way, but by simply being here in silence? It's marvelous to behold how the bodymind is disposing itself energetically, openly, without straining to do so—it is happening on its own. It is like a shift from watching a video to simply being present—awake, unencumbered, whole. No thought of loss or grief. No time.

LAUGHTER

Somebody asked: "What is the role of laughter in this work? Why don't we laugh more during retreat? Why does everybody look so serious?"

Can we let laughter do its own spontaneous thing? If we

are endeavoring to laugh because we think it is better than being serious, then it becomes contrived. We are steeped in that kind of humor—rarely does a speaker start without a joke or two so everybody laughs. It's considered a good thing to do. But in retreat nothing needs to be forced. Laughter happens spontaneously and heartily when we suddenly see ourselves in an astonishingly fresh light, not as the idealized character we imagined we were in our ongoing melodrama. There is nothing more hilarious than seeing our masquerade exposed!

5

Effort and Energy

P EOPLE FREQUENTLY EXPRESS dismay at experiencing endless streams of thought, even after sitting for many years: "Am I a hopeless case?" they ask. Or, "The mind is fairly quiet and spacious here at Springwater, but when I'm back home there is new entanglement again." Or, "How can I do it better, be more disciplined? I really have no discipline whatsoever. I lack a foundation, not having had any formal training. Do I need to make more of an *effort* to get thoughts under control, to become more concentrated to arrive at silence and understanding?"

When I talk about presence being effortless, not brought about by concentration, people sometimes will retort that I had many years of formal Zen training, so how can I say that this did not help me become more focused in the present? Actually, this mind was able to concentrate before starting Zen training. Concentration was never a problem. But being concentrated is not the same as being here, present, and clearly aware. We can practice concentration for years and become highly focused, even perform feats that seem miraculous. But does it help in understanding who we truly are, clearly, directly, beyond the shadow of doubt? It is hard to put it into words, but when this is clear, it is clear. It is not the product of concentration or imagination. I am not knocking concentration. It has its useful function in daily life, in arts, sciences, sports. In the kitchen, if I'm not concentrated the food will burn. Acrobats need enormous concentration to stay on the high wire, and so do bookkeepers to avoid making mistakes.

It is possible to learn to control the mind with practices like concentrating on the breath, a mantra, a mandala, a spot on the forehead or below the navel. This is concentrating by cutting off distractions. And what do we get in that process? Don't we get a concentrator, either a good or a bad one? The effort that comes from the thought of getting someplace or becoming something reinforces, in subtle ways, the sense of *me*. It reinforces the *me* as having to do something, being somebody, attaining something, or still lacking something. These are all ideas and images, deeply programmed and constantly reinforced in the human mind.

If anyone wishes to experiment with concentration, please do so. It is good training for the mind. But that training of the mind does not tell us what we are at this moment. What are we when there is no one doing anything, no one attaining anything, no place to go? There *is* no place to go. The whole foundation is already here in each one of us. It is the same in all of us. There is only one foundation, which is presence, wholeness, boundless love.

Can we come upon it?

It is always here. It has always been here. The concept of beginning and ending is time, produced by thought. Can we see right now that beginning and end, getting someplace, being somebody, wanting to get the something I lack are all products of the imagination? As long as this isn't clear, this bodymind remains tied up in knots. Can we see that thinking about tomorrow, or about what is planned for dinner tonight, is all conceptualization? We can think about food when there is actually no food in front of us. "Tonight" is a thought. "Dinner" is a thought. "The future," in which I will be enlightened, is a thought. Can we see it instantly? Can we see that a thought is always away from this present moment where time does not exist? When the food is right in front of us, are we just eating, or are we thinking about wanting more?

What are we really? Is that our real interest here? To come upon our true being, without deception, without kidding ourselves? Maybe we aren't interested in this. Some people have told me they have dropped the thought of getting enlightened, and all they are interested in now is being at ease, finding undisturbed quietness. They do not even want to be disturbed by a talk. A talk can be disturbing.

So our interests vary. And they may vary from one moment to the next. Here in this work of the moment we are not trying to mold ourselves to a preconceived path or "stages." Teachings that postulate stages grab the thinking mind. We wonder what these stages are like, and trying to figure them out is an exercise in headaches. Of course the main interest is, "What stage am *I* in? How many more will I have to go through?"

Can we drop the idea of stages and not pick it up again, even though it is prevalent in many traditions? Can we see and feel that any such conceptualization is already a straitjacket? Thought is so powerful—thinking what I am now, what I will be next, judging myself about what I think I am and what I could be. The power of such thoughts cannot be overestimated. They prevent a presence, an awareness that defies all definition.

We may think that effort is the source of awareness, but in presently awaring this thinking, there is no effort. It's just happening. Listen—rain is gently dropping on the roof, hitting the window panes, breath is flowing, crows are calling. We hear it clearly, don't we? Any effort?

Just because everything in this world seems to have a cause and an effect, there is a deeply lodged assumption that awareness too must have a cause, a deeper source. Is that so? Some people have found that doing a lot of sitting during a silent retreat results in greater awareness—the absence of self-consciousness and isolation. Do we conclude from this that long sitting causes awareness? When something as marvelous as openness, clarity, and lack of separation is palpably present, thought quickly tries to figure out what brought about this marvel, wondering: "What was I doing just before this happened? I must try to do that again." The brain is conditioned to assume that what happened before is responsible for what is going on now, and that *I* must have something to do with it!

So where does effort come into the work of this moment? "Work" is a loaded word. In the conditioned mind, it is associated with effort, goal, training, and getting rewards. Let us use the word "work" ever so lightly, carefully, for this meditative work is not work in the conventional sense that I have to make an effort to get someplace, attain something.

Over the years I have wondered what it is about silent retreats that seems to facilitate the emergence of openness, presence, and a simplicity of being. But it remains impossible to pin down any precipitating cause. We all know that time spent in motionless silence does not necessarily lead to a quiet mind.

All I can say at this moment of looking is that pure awareness is the silence of all habitual efforts to get someplace. It is the absence of any sense of me-in-time. In the past all kinds of efforts were made to learn to sit still over long periods of time, which undoubtedly played a part in learning to remain motionless in the midst of fear, pain, pleasure, and the restless desire to be somewhere else. Having the opportunity to sit quietly, over time, the bodymind is amazingly intelligent in learning new ways of being in the midst of the pushes and pulls of old habits. Habits are energies expended, but sitting quietly is energy gathering: awaring habits intelligently, letting them go without effort.

Some people ask if they should make more effort outside of retreat because they notice that two or three weeks after a retreat there is still some presence and spaciousness, but then the old compulsive patterns return. The mind then asks, "Could I make some special effort to keep that retreat awareness going in daily life?" We want to let the quietness and stillness savored in retreat flower in daily life. We want more quietness, less reactivity with people and situations. We want to do something to bring about more peacefulness and harmony. We ask ourselves how we can bring this about. We ask what effort can be undertaken, for it would be good not only for me but also for the world.

Do thoughts and desires for a better life for all of us take us away from the present moment—which may be rife with conflict and stress? Is it possible in the midst of the mess, the chaos, the suffering, to wake up and not immediately blame myself or others for being in it?

Rather than dreaming of a future world without chaos, can we be intimate with it as it is right now? Can we quiet down in the midst of the hurricane? There is a quiet spot at the center of each hurricane. It is called the eye. Can that eye be found right now?

Touching the eye may replace chaos with simple awareness, attention. Around the eye the debris may still be flying. Is that the challenge: finding the quiet eye of listening in the midst of chaos, beholding the whole thing even though it may not be pretty, blissful, or inspirational?

An anecdote comes to mind that I loved reading in the old Zen Center days. A monk named Wo Lun came to visit the Sixth Patriarch Hui Neng (who lived in China about twelve hundred years ago) to present his understanding to the master. This was the exchange:

Wo Lun:
Wo Lun has skillful means
Enabling him to cut off all thoughts.
In the face of circumstances
His mind is not aroused,
And daily, monthly, wisdom grows.

To which Hui Neng replied:
Hui Neng has no skillful means,
He does not cut off all thoughts.
In the face of circumstances
His mind is often aroused.
*So how can there be a growth of wisdom?**

For Hui Neng, there is just effortless, unselfconscious being. No time. When effortless being does not manifest directly, the *me* inevitably makes efforts to make progress. Effortless being means no *me* pushing for something, be it a quiet mind, enlightenment, wisdom, or anything else. Can the effort-ing *me* expose itself as an unnecessary and mostly

---

* From *The Sutra of the Sixth Patriarch on the Pristine Orthodox Dharma* (San Francisco: Buddha's Universal Church, 1964), p. 113.

disturbing thought? This exposure is *energy*—not effort—energy gathering in, not succumbing to wanting to get someplace else, but exploring what is right here, right now. Listening, being here, open, even though it may feel enclosed. Realizing the choicelessness of being here, even though the imagination wants to project "videos" of better places. Being here is not making an effort to relax or to find undisturbed quietness. If there is tension and disturbance, that is what is here.

Actually, what *is* here? Not defining it, not knowing it—listening and attending in a new way that is not teachable, not learnable.

It happens on its own, gathering energy, knowing nothing of effort.

6

The Authority of a Spiritual Teacher

*M*ANY OF US ARE deeply conditioned to seek out people of authority. Most of us grew up under the powerful wings of parents, caretakers, guardians, siblings, teachers, and all kinds of institutional and religious authorities. Even if our parents (or other authorities) were easygoing and permissive, they were immeasurably bigger and stronger than we were. From the beginning, they laid down the law in one way or another, meting out reward and punishment, and imprinting upon us what is "right" and what is "wrong." We grew up in the shelter or fear of their authority, and most of us came to believe that what our parents and elders did and said was the right thing to do and to say. This was not a deliberate choice on anyone's part—the grown-ups' conditioning became ours unconsciously. (I realize that not everyone grew up in the same way. A shelter of parental authority can easily turn into a prison, and the yearning for security flips into aversion and rebellion. What is of interest here is questioning and tracing our need for spiritual authority in a simple way.)

Spiritual teachers, with their prestige and power and the added ambiance of sanctity, bestow a great sense of inspiration, safety, and gratification upon us when we associate and identify with them, particularly if they look upon us benevolently or even think that we have promise. We feel blessed as though we had regained what we lost after childhood—someone to take care of us, to think and judge for us, direct us, expect high things from us, praise and blame us, and, in addition, know the mysterious ways of the "spirit." Becoming a student or disciple of such a teacher lends a heightened sense of importance and meaning and the hope of becoming like them some time in the future.

For a few years I was a teacher at a Zen center and, having known how it feels to be a student, I found it energizing and gratifying to be accepted as a Zen authority by others. Besides its difficulties and arduous work, it also created pleasures and conveniences. It felt good to be held in high esteem by others, to be spared scrutiny and criticism by one's students, to be served and attended to, to be listened and paid attention to as someone of special attainment and status. Thus teachers may garner from their exalted position feelings of superiority that can provide relief from inferiority feelings left over from childhood.

At the time of fulfilling the role of the teacher I noticed that the images students created of me and my images of them got in the way of direct, simple, unadorned communication with each other. With deepening awareness it was easy to see the artificial wraps in which people came into the meeting room, did their obligatory prostrations, and brought up their practice. Outside of formal meetings, there often was a veil over people's eyes as they looked, not at me, but at the image they had of me. This veil of imagery and ideas clouds our view of reality most of the time, as the brain has been an image maker since time immemorial. When you are thought of as a spiritual teacher, a few extras are added—you are seen not just as another human being but as somebody awesome, to be revered ("Your Reverence," "Your Holiness"), to be believed, worshiped, followed, and obeyed unconditionally.

I realized with increasing clarity that the essence of the work of this moment has nothing to do with upholding a revered tradition and its trappings but is rather concerned with seeing through them, seeing directly into the human mind beyond words and judgments. Carefully observing the habitual creation of images about each other, and having insight into their concealment of truth, is the beginning of wisdom. There is freedom in the very instant of direct discovery. Krishnamurti's work was of invaluable help in this. It became impossible for me to keep on with the outer and inner paraphernalia of being a Zen teacher, and I left it behind without protest, anger, or regrets. What mattered was to keep working with interested people in a way that did not perpetuate unnecessary ideas and belief systems but questioned them radically, shedding light on deeply ingrained habits. I ceased thinking of myself as a teacher and of people who came for this work as my students—a marvelous release into the naturalness of simple being. No one can teach anyone *the truth*, but can it be lived, expressed, and wondrously shared in direct insight.

What I say in retreat and write in books is not meant to establish any dogma or make myself into an authority. People have objected: "That's easy for you to say, but it's happening anyway." Well, if it's happening, can we be honestly curious about it and examine it? Not just theoretically thinking about it, but watching directly as the desire to believe in someone and become their follower wells up in the bodymind? Do we desire the safety of spiritual authority? Is there an urge to identity with someone of power and prestige? This may be an ambivalent thing—one wants it, and one also hates it; one fights it, and one also desires the comfort of believing and following what someone else says and does—it's so much easier than stopping, wondering, and looking for oneself!

The things that I say and write are not meant to influence or woo listeners and readers but to invite genuine curiosity and investigation. Everything that is pointed out here is open to questioning by each one of us. Nothing said is sacred or untouchable. I am not infallible. If you have questions or doubts, let's meet together and talk about it. If you disagree with what you heard me say, if you see things differently, if you want to go over the whole matter again or wish to go deeper, let's feel free to meet and talk together. There is no need to make anybody into an unquestioned authority or fight them just because we don't understand what they are saying, or because they are sitting in front of the hall and giving a talk. Can our inward reactions reveal themselves and be questioned in a simple way? Not understanding something is no calamity. Beginning to wonder about what sounds unthinkable becomes the source of inquiry and discovery. If we truly do not understand, can we let the incomprehensible percolate in wonderment throughout the heart, mind, and body?

In direct discovery, authority dissolves. We don't need anybody to tell us how things are when we see for ourselves. Nobody needs to teach us that it is raining when we feel wet drops moistening our skin. But often we don't see clearly, and in our confusion we blindly take over someone else's teaching, become identified with it, and defend it without questioning. That's not what this work is all about. Meditative inquiry is about looking together and alone, examining alone and together, and discovering the truth of this moment.

That happens in open listening and looking, free from the pressures of authority.

A few years ago someone said to me: "There seems to be some confusion about the word 'authority.' I don't come here to follow a teacher—I'm not interested in that. But I appreciate listening to someone who speaks with insight, strength of conviction, and presence. This for me is a person of authority." It is helpful to clear up what we mean by the words we are using, and I am grateful for such clarification.

Let me say a few words here about how I regard my function in this work of the moment. People have called it teacher, guide, facilitator, catalyst, mirror for seeing oneself. All of these different terms are appropriate in a way, but the simplicity of being here without any sense of separation and responding out of silent, empty listening cannot be captured in a definition. Defining oneself in any way harbors dangers. The human mind loves to grasp at concepts about itself, to feel good and important, as I have elaborated earlier in this chapter.

So if the work of this moment is not the transmission of something to someone—not the transmission of teachings, of traditional rituals, of secret or not-so-secret practices, not a body of knowledge or interpretations of scriptures—then what is it? What is my function in meeting with people who come in sorrow, confusion, anger, fear, despair, and a deep yearning to be healed, to become whole, to find out whether there is anything beyond the conflicts and sorrow of everyday life?

As the years go by I am learning more and more what it is *not*. The essential function of a spiritual guide is not, as I see it, to give instructions, practices, advice, solace, answers, solutions to problems, and so forth. It is rather to allow the total situation, as it is manifesting right now in us and around us, to reveal itself as it is and, if questioned about it, to point out as clearly as possible what is actually going on to whoever is interested in listening and looking. The spiritual guide's function is not just to talk out of remembrances of past experiences, not simply to use descriptions or give explanations, certainly not to "teach you." It is the complete entering into what is happening right here, lovingly, without any resistance, letting the meeting together percolate spontaneously—letting it all become transparent and express itself in words that arise freely, without hanging on to the words. Words can be changed. Nothing that is happening is permanent, and all is taking place in empty space without borders—"empty" meaning the absence of a self-centered network confining and fragmenting the space. When that network is in abeyance and the brain is awake, then there is the clarity to see people and things just as they are. In emptiness nothing collides with anything. Empty space does not resist the free movement of infinite happenings. In listening, speaking, and acting out of this common ground, we can awaken to the joy of wholeness—our true home.

7

Can This Work Be Transmitted?

QUESTION: I would like to ask you a question. I have deep respect for you—I've listened to your tapes and read your books. I also have deep respect for the others present here, and for myself. We have been talking a lot about the future of Buddhism in America, and many people here are from different traditions, and some are not affiliated with traditions. Generally the traditions have a concept of transmission and lineage—lineage from master to teacher to support the tradition down through the centuries and support the teachings that will succeed us. Your discovery, your approach is seen by many people as a stripping away of form, and I think many people would see something of the future of Buddhism in a form that has no form, that asks, as you do, that you be simply present with the moment. As a person grounded in the traditions, I'm asking whether you could address my concerns about the future, about future developments *without* a sense of lineage.

Adapted from a question-and-answer session at the Buddhism in America Conference, Boston, January 1997.

TONI PACKER: Truth itself needs no lineage. It is here, without past or future. I cannot share your concerns for the future because I don't have them.

I am always interested in what people say, feel, fear, and creatively imagine, and I'm curious about what is being envisioned for Springwater, but I'm not concerned about the future. I'm saying this completely honestly. From its very beginnings, which cannot even be remembered, this whole amazing unfolding of inquiry and discovery in silent space has completely taken care of itself in an unfathomable way. Shall we now worry about how it will continue? Even though I have been well acquainted with fear and worry about an uncertain future, or rather an uncertain *present*, since my early childhood days in Nazi Germany, I feel a total absence of this apprehension with regard to the work we do at Springwater. I understand the brain's ingrained occupation with thoughts and plans about future developments—it certainly has a practical function in daily life. But it is a wondrous happening when creative responses arise out of the openness of simply being here this moment, awake, and empty of self-interest—no felt need to identify with any person, place, group, or teaching. How could anyone be worried that truth might not reveal itself entirely on its own at any moment? It's doing it all the time! Truth doesn't need a midwife to come into being.

"Transmission" takes place when two people, or a group of people, see completely eye to eye—one single eye seeing. I'm not talking of sharing the same opinions or traditions, but of being free from conditioned opinions and traditions at the instant of seeing. When the tight enclosure of self-delusion becomes luminously transparent, narrowness is replaced by vastness—there is no one here to be anything, nothing to get, nothing to know, nothing to pass on. What is there to transmit? To whom? We're not divided from each other! I give you a hug. Did I transmit love to you? Or is it here, flowering joyously?

I do remember koans from Zen training that dealt with "preserving the house and the gate"—the house and the gate referring not just to the temple but to the entire tradition. The budding Zen teacher going through koans has to learn not only to speak and act before the teacher out of "nonduality" but also to take on the responsibility of preserving and perpetuating the house and gate of their lineage. That's not what I'm interested in. I wish for Springwater to flourish in its own spontaneous and unpredictable ways and not become a place for the transmission of traditional teachings. But if this should happen, so be it. We can wake up at any time!

Am I communicating with you? Have I been talking to your question?

Q: Yes. If you had put the question to me, "What is it that is transmitted?" I could talk to that question, but I'm here to listen. In a sense there is a body of knowledge that is intuitive, that seems actually—

TP: Yeah—that I leave to others.

Q: A master will have presence. You yourself have a state of presence. If you were not present yourself but spoke to others continually *about* presence, I think the respect that you deserve, and that you receive, would not be there. So there is something that you are transmitting that isn't just words.

TP: Is there something? (*Pause.*) Yes!

Q: Your presence is first, to those who are—

TP: It's not mine, it's not mine! *(Laughter.)* Or is it?

Q: No, it's not yours. It's not yours, it's not mine, it's not ours, it is *presence.*

TP: Yes, yes! And who transmits it to whom? Who "receives" it when it's simply here?

Q: When one is deluded, and one is not clear . . .

TP: Yes?

Q: . . . then there is a transmission.

TP: *(laughs)* Yes! You said it! I didn't. *(Laughter.)*

Q: It's hard for me to say that it doesn't happen. Say I'm in the presence of a master, and I am deluded, and gradually through the collapse of my strategies I fall into the presence of the master. The master is skillful, and I have experienced that as a transmission, so it's difficult for me to say that it hasn't happened. I began by saying, out of respect for you, that I ask these questions, and it is really out of deep respect—I'm not trying to set traps.

TP: I didn't feel that you did. What is there to get trapped?

Q: I know it sounds like I'm only trying to be clever with you, and I'm not—

TP: No, I understand.

Q: I'm just being with you. It's a privilege, rather than just listening to your voice on a tape.

TP: Here is the real thing!

Q: Is there a possibility of all of us learning the same truth through different paths?

TP: We learn the truth *in spite* of different paths! Truth has nothing to do with a path. I'm not saying this facetiously.

Q: No, I hear you.

TP: Truth is not caused by a path. And waking up—who knows why there is waking up? It's the miracle of humanity, or of the universe, that there is waking up to the truth of infinite wholeness! For me to think that you woke up because my tradition did something for you can make me feel good about myself and about my tradition.

If I remember correctly, the Buddha once said: "Since there is the Unbecome, the Unborn, the Unmade and Un-formed, there can be liberation from the Become, the Born, the Made and Formed." *Unbecome* means not subject to cause and effect. Everything we do—striving, hurting, retaliating, or forgiving each other—is the conditioned stuff of cause and effect. The clarity of insight is unconditioned—it has no cause and no effect.

Why "no effect"?

If you belittle me, and there is complete listening, com-plete attention to what you're saying—what's going on for you and what's happening in me, to the body's impulse to tighten up, fight back, defend itself, or withdraw in pain—if there is complete openness in listening, attending to the whole thing vulnerably, innocently, then what you are saying need not become the cause of an effect.

I see you're nodding. You understand.

People say to me: "Didn't you, Toni, learn to concentrate and be aware through long years of Zen practice—wasn't that the cause of an effect?" And looking back through mem-ory, I can say, yes, twenty, thirty years ago, there wasn't this ability to look and attend quietly, undividedly, in a sustained way. But one also realizes that uncountable other things, beside Zen training, have fed into the unfolding of this present moment, including the Big Bang, the fact that the universe happened at all. If it becomes clear that right now we're the result of everything that's ever happened, why pick out one thing and say *that* was the cause of *this?* Everything is the cause of everything, and everything is also the effect of everything. And yet—this moment of being here completely unfettered is timeless and without cause.

Someone asked me, "Can a leaf swirling to the ground be my teacher?" Yes! Of course! This instant of seeing is the timeless teacher, the leaves are just what they are.

Q: You're pointing to awareness, not to a method, if I've understood correctly. I'm reflecting back, "What is awareness?" and in a sense it isn't a practice. Awareness is what it is, it's not a practice. Am I echoing what you said, or am I distorting?

What I wanted to put to you was, we came to your talk from listening to Tsultrim speaking about the three vehicles with the vast array of practices. Everybody was listening to the vast array of practices. Pointing to awareness is staying with the essence, if you like, the very essence, but people go through a vast array of different states and problems. I've heard the Dalai Lama say about certain Zen schools, "They have one method." Is one method enough to cope with all the various types of problems and states that people have? Pointing to awareness is not even in essence a method. I understand that. I wonder if you could address that for me.

TP: What are you asking?

Q: The vast array of methods in Buddhism—ah, you're not even really advocating *one method!*

TP: No. And yet we work. We look and listen, just as we're doing right now. If you say that's a method, well, I don't care what words you use. We love to label things, don't we? People say to me, "You have the 'methodless method,'" and stuff like that. *(Laughter.)*

But I have no quarrels, I'm not fighting people who do practices. I don't know. See, insight happens. In spite of anything we do, it does happen.

Several years ago, a man came to Springwater who wanted to talk to me about an experience he had during the Vietnam War. I had never seen him before, nor did he ever come back. He looked somewhat unpolished; he told me he was a steelworker. The memory of that day in Vietnam had just come up again, and he wanted to talk to somebody who might understand. This is how I remember his story: In Vietnam, not too far from where his platoon was located, there was a hill dangerously "infested" with Vietcong fighters, and his commander was charged with capturing that hill from the air. He asked for volunteers, but nobody volunteered. So individual names were called up, and his was among them. "You cannot possibly imagine how I felt," he told me. "My knees were shaking so fiercely I hardly made it up to the helicopter. I was in total panic." And then, flying and looking for that hill, something inconceivable happened. Suddenly every bit of fear dropped away and there was nothing but vastness and peace and joy and love—these may not have been his exact words, but that was the essence. "And," he added, "we didn't even find that hill—it didn't exist." Returning to his unit, he was overflowing with the urge to tell people what had happened to him, but his buddies just laughed at him. Maybe they thought he was off, that something had snapped in him. He told his wife later, and she didn't understand either.

So—a flash of insight happens to a frightened marine on a death raid in a helicopter. We could say that maybe facing death caused everything to drop away. And when everything drops away, all the paths, the refuges, the "I am" and the "Buddha, Dharma, Sangha"—what's left?

When the fog lifts, bright sunshine illuminates and warms the whole earth.

So, you see, I'm not really concerned with practices and paths. I understand that you are, because you may be in the midst of all this right now. We can start working together from scratch at any time, but if you do something else, then you do something else. It doesn't matter much, does it?

PART TWO

Me and You and the World

8

What Is the Me?

A SOMBER DAY, isn't it? Dark, cloudy, cool, moist, and windy. Amazing, this whole affair of the weather!

We call it weather, but what is it really? Wind. Rain. Clouds slowly parting. Not the words spoken about it, but just this darkening, blowing, pounding, wetting, and then lightening up, blue sky appearing amid darkness, and sunshine sparkling on wet grasses and leaves. In a little while there'll be frost, snow, and ice covers. And then warming again, melting, oozing water everywhere. On an early spring day the dirt road sparkles with streams of wet silver. So— what is weather other than this incessant change of earthly conditions and all the human thoughts, feelings, and undertakings influenced by it? Like and dislike. Depression and elation. Creation and destruction. An ongoing, ever changing stream of happenings abiding nowhere. No real entity *weather* exists anywhere except in thinking and talking about it.

Now, is there such an entity as *me* or *I*? Or is it just like the weather—an ongoing, ever changing stream of ideas, images, memories, projections, likes and dislikes, creation and destruction, that thought keeps calling *I, me, Toni,* and thereby solidifying what is evanescent? What am I really, truly, and what do I merely think and believe I am?

Are we interested in exploring this amazing affair of *myself* from moment to moment? Is this, maybe, the essence of this work? Exploring ourselves attentively beyond the peace and quiet that we are seeking and maybe finding occasionally? Coming upon an amazing insight into this deep sense of separation that we call *me and other people, me and the world*, without any need to condemn or overcome?

Most human beings take it for granted that I am *me*, and that *me* is this body, this mind, this knowledge and sense of myself that feels so obviously distinct and separate from other people and from the nature around us. The language in which we talk to ourselves and to each other inevitably implies separate *me*s and *you*s all the time. All of us talk *I-and-you* talk. We think it, write it, read it, and dream it with rarely any pause. There is incessant reinforcement of the sense of *me*, separate from others. Isolated, insulated *me*. Not understood by others. How are we to come upon the truth if separateness is taken so much for granted, feels so commonsense?

The difficulty is not insurmountable. Wholeness, our true being, is here all the time, like the sun behind the clouds. Light is here in spite of cloud cover.

What makes up the clouds?

Can we begin to realize that we live in conceptual, abstract ideas about ourselves? That we are rarely in touch directly with what actually is going on? Can we realize that thoughts about myself—I'm good or bad, I'm liked or disliked—are nothing but thoughts, and that thoughts do not tell us the truth about what we really are? A thought is a thought, and it triggers instant physical reactions, pleasures and pains throughout the bodymind. Physical reactions generate further thoughts and feelings about myself—"I'm suffering," "I'm happy," "I'm not as bright, as good looking as the others." That feedback implies that all this is *me*, that I have gotten hurt, or feel good about myself, or that I need to defend myself or get more approval and love from others. When we're protecting ourselves in our daily interrelationships we're not protecting ourselves from flying stones or bomb attacks. It's from words we're taking cover, from gestures, from coloration of voice and innuendo.

"We're protecting ourselves, we're taking cover." In using our common language the implication is constantly created that there is someone real who is protecting and someone real that needs protection.

Is there someone real to be protected from words and gestures, or are we merely living in ideas and stories about me and you, all of it happening in the ongoing audio/video drama of ourselves?

The utmost care and attention is needed to see the internal drama fairly accurately, dispassionately, in order to express it as it is seen. What we mean by "being made to feel good" or "getting hurt" is the internal enhancing of our ongoing *me*-story, or the puncturing and deflating of it. Enhancement or disturbance of the *me*-story is accompanied by pleasurable energies or painful feelings and emotions throughout the organism. Either warmth or chill can be felt at the drop of a word that evokes memories, feelings, passions. Conscious or unconscious emotional recollections of what happened yesterday or long ago surge through the bodymind, causing feelings of happiness or sadness, affection or humiliation.

Right now words are being spoken, and they can be followed literally. If they are fairly clear and logical they can make sense intellectually. Perhaps at first it's necessary to understand intellectually what is going on in us. But that's not completely understanding the whole thing. These words point to something that may be *directly* seen and felt, inwardly, as the words are heard or read.

As we wake up from moment to moment, can we experience freshly, directly, when hurt or flattery is taking place?

What is happening? What is being hurt? And what keeps the hurt going?

Can there be some awareness of defenses arising, fear and anger forming, or withdrawal taking place, all accompanied by some kind of story line? Can the whole drama become increasingly transparent? And in becoming increasingly transparent, can it be thoroughly questioned? What is it that is being protected? What is it that gets hurt or flattered? *Me?* What is *me?* Is it images, ideas, memories?

It is amazing. A spark of awareness witnessing how one spoken word arouses pleasure or pain throughout the body-mind. Can the instant connection between thought and sensations become palpable? The immediacy of it. No *I*-entity directing it, even though we say and believe I am doing all that. It's just happening automatically, with no one intending to "do" it. Those are all afterthoughts!

We say, "I didn't want to do that," as though we could have done otherwise. Words and reaction proceed along well-oiled pathways and interconnections. A thought about the loss of a loved one comes up and immediately the solar plexus tightens in pain. Fantasy of lovemaking occurs and an ocean of pleasure ensues. Who does all that? Thought says, "I do. I'm doing that to myself."

To whom is it happening? Thought says, "To me, of course!"

But where and what is this *I*, this *me*, aside from all the thoughts and feelings, the palpitating heart, the painful and pleasurable energies circulating throughout the organism?

Who could possibly be doing it all with such amazing speed and precision? Thinking about ourselves and the triggering of physiological reactions takes time, but present awareness brings the whole drama to light instantly. Everything is happening on its own. No one is directing the show!

Right at this moment wind is storming, windows are rattling, tree branches are creaking, and leaves are quivering. It's all here in the listening—but whose listening is it? Mine? Yours? We say, "I'm listening," or, "I cannot listen as well as you do," and these words befuddle the mind with feelings and emotions learned long ago. You may be protesting, "My hearing isn't yours. Your body isn't mine." We have thought like that for eons and behave accordingly; but at this moment can there be just the sound of swaying trees and rustling leaves and fresh air from the open window cooling the skin? It's not happening to anyone. It's simply present for all of us, isn't it?

Do I sound as though I'm trying to convince you of something? The passion arising in trying to communicate simply, clearly, may be misunderstood for a desire to influence people. That's not the case. There is just the description of what is happening here for all of us. Nothing needs to be sold or bought. Can we simply listen and investigate what is being offered for exploration from moment to moment?

What is the *me* that gets hurt or flattered, time and time again, the world over? In psychological terms we say that we are identified with ourselves. In spiritual language we say that we are attached to ourselves. What is this *ourselves?* Is it feeling of myself existing, knowing what I am, having lots of recollections about myself—all the ideas and pictures and feelings about myself strung together in a coherent story? And knowing this story very well—multitudes of memories, some added, some dropped, all interconnected—what I am, how I look, what my abilities and disabilities are, my education, my family, my name, my likes and dislikes, opinions, beliefs, and so on. The identification with all of that, which says, "This is what I am." And the attachment to it, which says, "I can't let go of it."

Let's go beyond concepts and look directly into what we mean by them. If one says, "I'm identified with my family name," what does that mean? Let me give an example. As a growing child I was very much identified with my last name because it was my father's and he was famous—so I was told. I liked to tell others about my father's scientific achievements to garner respect and pleasurable feelings for myself by impressing friends. I felt admiration through other people's eyes. It may not even have been there. It may have been projected. Perhaps some people even felt, "What a bore she is!" On the entrance door to our apartment there was a little polished brass plate with my father's name engraved on it and his titles: "Professor Doctor Phil." The "Phil" impressed me particularly, because I thought it meant that my father was a philosopher, which he was not. I must have had the idea that a philosopher was a particularly imposing personage. So I told some of my friends about it and brought them to look at the little brass sign at the door.

This is one meaning of identification—enhancing one's sense of self by incorporating ideas about other individuals or groups, or one's possessions, achievements, transgressions—anything—and feeling that all of this is *me*. Feeling important about oneself generates amazingly addictive energies.

To give another example from the past: I became very identified with my half-Jewish descent. Not openly in Germany, where I mostly tried to hide it rather than display it, but later on after the war ended, telling people of our family's fate and finding welcome attention, instant sympathy, and nourishing interest in the story. One can become quite addicted to making the story of one's life impressive to others and to oneself, and feed on the energies aroused by that. And when that sense of identification and attachment is disturbed by someone not buying into it, contesting it, or questioning it altogether, there is sudden insecurity, physical discomfort, anger, fear, and hurt.

Becoming a member of a Zen center and engaging in spiritual practice, I realized one day that I had not been talking about my background in a long while. And now, when somebody brings it up—sometimes an interviewer will ask me to talk about it—it feels like so much bother and effort. Why delve into old memory stuff? I want to talk about listening, the wind, and the birds.

Are we listening right now? Or are we more interested in identities and stories?

We all love stories, don't we? Telling them and hearing them is wonderfully entertaining.

At times people wonder why I don't call myself a teacher when I'm so obviously engaged in teaching. Somebody actually brought it up this morning—the projections and the associations aroused in waiting outside the meeting room and then entering nervously with a pounding heart. Do images of teacher and student offer themselves automatically like clothes to put on and roles to play in these clothes? In giving talks and meeting with people the student-teacher imagery does not have to be there—it belongs to a different level of existence. If images do come up, they're in the way, like clouds hiding the sun. Relating without images is the freshest, freest thing in the universe.

So, what am I and what are you—what are we without images clothing and hiding our true being? It's un-imageinable, isn't it? And yet there's the sound of wind blowing, trees shaking, crows cawing, woodwork creaking, breath flowing without need for any thoughts. Thoughts are grafted on top of what's actually going on right now, and in that grafted world we happen to spend most of our lives.

Yet every once in a while, whether one does meditation or not, the real world shines wondrously through everything. How is it when words fall silent? When there is no knowing? When there is no listener and yet there is listening, awaring in utter silence?

The listening to, the awaring of the *me*-story is not part of the *me*. Awareness is not part of that network. The network cannot witness itself. It can think about itself and even change itself, establish new behavior patterns, but it cannot see itself or free itself. There is a whole psychological science called behavior modification that, through reward and punishment, tries to drop undesirable habits and adopt better, more sociable ones. This is not what we're talking about. The seeing, the awaring of the *me* movement is not part of the *me* movement.

A moment during a visit with my parents in Switzerland comes to mind. I had always had a difficult relationship with my mother. I had been afraid of her. She was a very passionate woman with lots of anger, but also love. Once during that visit I saw her standing in the dining room facing me. She was just standing there, and for no known reason I suddenly saw her without the past. There was no image of her, and also no idea of what she saw in me. All that was gone. There was nothing left except pure love for this woman. Such beauty shone out of her. And our relationship changed; there was a new closeness. No one changed it. It just happened.

Truly seeing is freeing beyond imagination.

9

Personality

*E*ARLIER THIS MORNING when I left the house, the sky was dark and cloudy, and the fields, the hills, and the road were almost colorless, without shine. And then this ever new miracle unfolded: the clouds parted, patches of blue appeared, and the sun came pouring through, lighting up the world, making the snow sparkle and the sky, hills, and houses shine with fresh light. A flock of crows flew across the road, very black and active, setting off the tenderness of the landscape.

Who would have thought this morning when waking up to darkness, winds, and drifting snow, to colorless tree lines and fields, that this sudden transformation could happen? But it did, and it does, and the clouds will also pull together again and new clouds arrive that hide the sun and drain the color out of the world.

What I want to talk about this morning is personality— the individual person. Let's talk about that because it is a source of error for most of us most of the time. I am calling it a source of error because personality is a mistaken identity. Particularly in our Western civilization there is a strong identification with our personality, and we identify other people by theirs. The brain creates images about other persons that are remembered and projected like concealing screens: images about myself, images of the others referring to their personalities. I say *mistaken identities* because we are so deeply, emotionally convinced that this is what we are and what others are.

It's a deep conviction that is not even questioned except in some spiritual circles. We are convinced that we know what we are because we are conscious of ourselves. By being conscious I mean that we think about ourselves a good deal of the time in pictures, in stories composed about remembered experiences and all the psychological knowledge the brain has accumulated over the years.

New sense impressions coming in from other persons are immediately transmitted to the brain and interpreted, associated, and judged there in terms of past recorded memories: what I have known about that person, who and what they remind me of are quickly projected onto that other person. When this is happening we do not see someone as they are right now—we see the memories and judgments projected by the brain. All this can become transparent in awareness.

We are habitually absorbed in our ideas and judgments about each other and are little aware of the actual moment-to-moment happenings between us. It feels so true that you are what I know you to be, and that I am what I know about myself. We don't realize easily that what I think I am is to a large extent the picture-story about myself. I can think endlessly about the characteristics of my body, its looks and its needs, my name, my age, my inherited qualities, my parents, my history, my experiences, my artistic, mathematical, or athletic talents and potential I think I have. And there is a reaction to everything I think about myself—I like it or I don't, I want to get rid of it or keep it forever.

So we become identified with our characteristics and abili-

ties and identify others by theirs. There is a feeling of owner-
ship here: We think we are the owners of our traits, our
personalities, our bodies, our knowledge, and our opinions.
And we feel that we deserve to be what we are as though we
ourselves had brought it about. "I have worked hard on myself," we like to say. The working hard on oneself is also part
of our personality. When we feel that we haven't accomplished anything worthwhile in our life, we feel responsible
for the failure—it's our own fault if we don't amount to
anything. Can we look at all this and question it thoroughly?

In my delusion I feel that somehow I have brought myself
about the way I am, that I own what I have become, and that
I can get better if I put my mind to it and work on myself
with determination and willpower. I also believe that other
people should do the same thing. We somehow feel it's their
fault that they are the way they are. Finding fault is part of
our relationship with each other—blaming each other openly
or tacitly for what we are, what we have done or what we
don't do.

A memory comes to mind about Kyle, my late husband.
He grew up in a puritanical family and was raised to be
modest and honest, imbued with a strong drive for bettering
himself. The idea of improving himself, of becoming a better
person, was a strong motive in his family. Then one day—he
must have been in his fifties—we visited Ojai in California
and sat in the Oak Grove listening to Krishnamurti talk
about human beings' everlasting endeavors to become something or somebody in the future. As soon as the talk was
over, I saw Kyle jumping up and coming toward me with a
lightness of energy that was quite unusual for him. He
laughed heartily and exclaimed, "Here I've been attempting
to become a better person all my life—ha ha ha ha ha!" He
beamed with joy and didn't describe anything more, because

direct insight is indescribable. It is that wondrous state of being in which the conditioned personality reveals itself for what it is—conditioning giving way to wholeness without lack, all things and people, mountains and oak trees being wondrously the way they are, nothing to be faulted, nothing to be improved.

That realization stayed with Kyle, even though, with his terminal illness and under the influence of many different medications, there were occasional surprising shifts in his personality. He could temporarily become disagreeable, demanding, and self-righteous, which was so totally out of character. One time he said with sadness, "I haven't really accomplished anything in my life." "You are here! That's all that matters," I replied. He must have understood because he never brought it up again.

Our personality is not reliable and not for keeps. It is changeable like the weather and disappears when the body dies. During our lifetime we may try to change it with great resolve and effort and maybe get some results, but they can easily fall apart again when our body and situation change or old temptations arise.

Can there be insight into our lifelong conditioned patterns, how we repeatedly react to irritations with anger, fear, frustration, and defensiveness? And then the subsequent dismay and regret that we are *still* so reactive in spite of having done a lot of sitting! We think that we ought to be able to overcome our shortcomings if we only do enough sitting. That is why it is so important to understand, maybe at first intellectually, that our personality is a deeply wired pattern produced by uncountable past influences, which firmly resist our desire to change them. Personality has evolved from DNA, genes, family history, social conditions, culture, and myriad factors that cannot possibly be known and traced. But is it truly what we are?

Most of us don't even come across spiritual teachings about our true being as long as we are totally identified and absorbed with ourselves. We plod along in ignorance, at times appearing successful, and then again caught up in disillusionment and frustration, feeling despair and isolation. Again we may recover, perhaps with the help of therapy, which can be beneficial for wounded egos. When we think we are falling apart, a therapist can help to put Humpty Dumpty together again, making us feel more at home again in our healed personality. But then there may come a moment when we realize that nothing has really helped fundamentally. "I've been trying to improve myself all my life," says Kyle with cheerful laughter, "and to no avail!" All these attempts were instantly seen as false.

When we truly reach a dead end we may suddenly come across a teaching, a human being, a tape, or a book that radiates a joyous presence and awareness—a freedom unlinked to personality. The amazing and rationally inexplicable thing is that when we find ourselves at the end of the rope we come across a book, or someone alive who stuns, even shocks our entire being: everything that we have believed to be so may not really be true!

When we first experience this shakeup we may quickly reject it—we don't want to hear more about it. It doesn't really make logical sense. It's too threatening to the ego. And as long as the ego process dominates the moment, truth can't be properly understood—it is misunderstood as a threat to the *me*. But even if this is our first reaction, something unresolved and nagging is left tumbling around in the mind. The words one heard, the astonishment one experienced are not completely forgotten. It all comes to the fore again at a new moment of emergency. *Emergency*—what a beautiful word! It doesn't just mean emergency room, accident, earthquake, or flood, but the *emergence* of something entirely new this moment.

What emerges is a real yearning to find out whether what I've read and heard or seen in someone is actually realizable in myself. That question comes alive—not just an intellectual comprehension but a deep wondering whether verbal, theoretical understanding is all there is. "What are those words pointing at? Where is that person coming from to say such amazingly resonating things? Is there something other than what I have known up until now?" And with that we enter into a new wondering: "What am I beyond all that I know about myself?" Questions take different forms for different people. One need not adopt one artificially. Genuine questions emerge on their own when we begin to wonder about what we have taken for granted all our life.

With the energy of questioning, there is a breakup in the cloudy sky—a breaking into awareness of habitual reactions. No longer just being totally identified with them and becoming defensive about them, but really wondering about our moment-to-moment behavior, observing it with sparks of awareness. Throwing light on these incredible patterns in which we live—the self-protective patterns.

Self-protection is our strongest reaction pattern—it seems to be programmed into every cell of a living being in order to maintain, defend, and perpetuate itself. It is the essence of the life program and is also functioning within our elaborate *me*-structure. The entire *me*-structure demands to be protected and perpetuated as though it were a living being. The moment somebody says something critical about me, the instant reflex of preservation, defense, and aggression springs into action.

What is actually getting hurt by someone's critical remark to demand such instant protection? What is being protected with our instant defensive reaction? The automatic answer may be: "Me! I got hurt by what she said." And then an elaboration: "I need to defend myself or else people will walk all over me, take advantage of me, abuse me." But in this work of meditative inquiry, automatic answers will no longer do. What exactly is this *me* that feels hurt right now? Is it something real, or is it just an image that got "damaged" and now hurts mentally as well as physically? It's amazing to discover that a hurt image can make the entire bodymind ache physically.

All of this can be questioned with a fresh curiosity when we are not totally identified with our automatic reactions. How amazing is the energy to protect myself, or to blame others for what is happening to me, to project onto others what I don't dare see in myself! Other people appear defensive if I don't see my own defensiveness. But if I patiently witness defensiveness as it is unfolding in the mind, I also understand your defending yourself and needn't react to it. There is a recognition: this is how it feels right now for this person—the embarrassment, the anger, the anxiety, the contortion to protect something that doesn't even exist. Change can happen when awareness takes the place of ignorance.

Do we realize that no matter how precious personality is to us, it is perfectly all right to question and shed light on it? It's perfectly all right to wonder whether this is all there is to *me* and to *you*. Then maybe, to one's utter surprise, there is a moment of *emergency* when the response doesn't come out of the self-protective pattern, or that of finding fault with others. It emerges out of the wholeness of seeing this present moment. Not just images of *me* and *you*. Awareness illuminates, and a wise response emerges that is unpremeditated.

The brain immediately wants to appropriate this moment of freedom and make it into a prescription: "How can I bring it about again? What was I doing right before this happened?" We are mistaken to assume that the wisdom and love of wholeness can be captured and controlled by the ego. It isn't part of our personality! It's what we are when personality is in abeyance.

Zen teacher Hui Neng said over a thousand years ago:

> *One enlightened moment, and an ordinary man is a Buddha.*
> *One deluded moment, and a Buddha is an ordinary man.**

Or person, if you will.

---

*Exact source of these lines is unknown.

10

Touching Fear

L ET'S LOOK AT FEAR—maybe it is one of the most troublesome knots in our lives. Looking directly at fear is the same as looking undividedly at anger or hurt, at pain, greed, jealousy, envy, or pleasure. What unites all these states of the mind and body is the simple beholding when they manifest—the complete awaring with nothing held back. Being with it all without a hairbreadth of separation. Even though language designates different mind states and a *me* who "has" them and can be with them, being with anything simply means no separation—the whole thing taking place with nothing left over. Fear happening in simple awareness. No story needed to frame it.

There is so much fear in our lives, both conscious and unconscious. It comes up again and again, inundating the entire organism, particularly during retreat, when there is a lessening of resistance. "I'm never free of fear," some people say, implying that there should be a state of mind and body that is free from fear. How can we possibly be free from fear when we live in the conditioned mode of the *me*-story most of the time? We're deeply programmed to believe in this separate *me* by inaccurate language and by growing up in a world of other *me*s, all of whom think of and experience themselves as separate entities.

With separation inevitably goes fear and pain. It has been wired into us throughout the millennia, through remembered or repressed trauma, through traditions, teachings, through the way our parents were brought up and bring us up with them. Learning to be afraid of God or gods, of punishment, lack of love, loss, sickness, and death. Afraid of what we are doing to each other and what we might be doing to each other in the future. Deeply afraid of getting killed in the little wars and the big wars. Afraid of the sorrow human beings have endured since time immemorial, and afraid of its endless repetition.

Then there are all the fears of doing something wrong, of having done something bad, the fear of things going wrong with this incredibly delicate organism that we say is ours. It's not ours. It's simply alive. It unfolds within this world and lives and dies with it. It's so indescribably delicate, so fragile.

Right at this moment a dear friend of mine is being operated on for a brain tumor. A twelve-hour operation involving a team of surgeons is taking place right now, along with hundreds and thousands of other surgeries. A young man full of energy, full of creativity and love is at great risk of not continuing to live. How perishable we are regardless of our age.

As long as we don't think about it, we may not feel fear at this moment. Then as thoughts arise about someone close to us who is ill, or as we imagine being ill like that ourselves, the fear mode goes into gear. It is inevitably intertwined with an existence that believes itself to be separate from everyone and everything else, separate from life as a whole. The last words I said to the friend over the phone before his surgery were: "I can't say 'you'll be all right,' because you *are* all right!" It was not meant as a word of comfort. We are all right as we are in sickness, in health, or on the death bed.

The thinking brain is programmed to project each one of us as leading a separate existence, having to struggle for ourselves, maintain ourselves, fight for ourselves, protect ourselves. At times we feel the exuberance of being successful, yet underneath, the fear reflex hovers, ready to spring into action at any time. No matter how well defended we may be in a tightly protective cocoon, it's still just a thought-created enclosure harboring fear.

Fear ceases the moment the cocoon cracks open. There simply is no one here. No cocoon! Separation is like a bad dream. Upon waking up there is no need to struggle for or against others, for the common good or against a common evil. Everything is taking place in its own mysterious way. We don't have to do anything to make the shadow play happen. It happens by itself!

Without a cocoon there is no fear. Fear doesn't exist in the instant of freedom from the conditioned *me*-network. Dreaming about me versus the world only happens inside the cocoon. The cocoon is the world of dreams, and fear is part and parcel of it. So how to deal with it? Because this is what we want to learn, isn't it—how to deal with fear?

Fear arises and takes over the bodymind. A thought or a wordless memory has triggered it, and here it is. It feels highly unpleasant. Have you ever felt it completely, wordlessly, without stopping in the middle? For a long time I did not really feel fear, not daring to be in direct touch with it. It was there, lurking, but it wasn't completely felt because there was an unquestioned notion operating in the bodymind that it shouldn't be felt—I shouldn't feel painful things, I should stay away from them. Guard against them because they signal great danger. Grow a thick impenetrable skin that avoids feeling it. Which is like an organism's response against "foreign bodies." The body encapsulates toxic bodies that enter it. There's a lot of encapsulation happening within us, physiologically and psychologically, sealing off painful experiences so they become inaccessible to present sensing and feeling. *Almost* inaccessible, because they still linger and fester somewhere.

So here is a deep, underlying assumption that I mustn't touch terrible, horrible feelings. Have you come upon this assumption in quiet sitting? It's there in all of us. And we're questioning it right now. Questioning the very resistance that comes up automatically when something painful is taking place—resisting feeling it intimately. Aren't we familiar with the resistance to disturbing sensations? Resistance manifests as tightening in the stomach, the heart, the intestines, the muscles. Whatever it is, can we sense it thoroughly, not move away from it? Nothing can truly hurt us except denying or escaping from what is here as it is.

Right now I've been naming symptoms of resistance because we're talking with each other, but quietly by myself I needn't label anything that is felt. Just be completely in touch with this wholly indivisible moment of aliveness. It is an entirely new event. No resistance. No bracing against what is happening. Not knowing it from the past. Not assuming it is something dangerous, something to be avoided. Not knowing. Not knowing is the truth—we do not know. Just let everything be here, fully experienced from beginning to end. Let it unfold on its own. It needs no help from me—it is Life. Krishnamurti used to say, "Let it flower. Let the jealousy flower!" Somebody objected, "How can I let jealousy flower? It is so destructive!" "Look at it like a jewel in your hand," he replied.

Let's drop the metaphor and come back to the immediacy

of fear stirring. Feel it so choicelessly that all separation drops away! There is no *fear*, no one who has it, no one who suffers it, no one who made me afraid. Whatever is going on is just here—beckoning to unfold and dissolve in empty space. Isn't that what every feeling and sensation does? It comes into being, unfolds, and withers away without leaving a trace unless kept going by the fuel of thought and remembrance.

Are we ready for this? Will we remember it next time? This time! The habit is so strong to push the unpleasant aside. No need to make a big deal out of it. It isn't a big deal. Something comes up and is immediately allowed to be there, to be seen and felt without a break. Let it have the space it needs to unfold. Let it say what it needs to say. The sound of an airplane and the touch of a gentle breeze are here too. The birds are singing. The breath is flowing, maybe haltingly. In quietly being with everything there is hardly any breathing at all. And then a deep breath because the organism needs fresh oxygen.

No separation! Just the touching and wondering—the listening and looking without knowing. Then it is all happening in vast space, full of energy and love. In the listening and wondering, things become coherent, understandable, light. Too marvelous to put into words.

11

Anger

LET'S TALK ABOUT ANGER. Everyone experiences it in controlled or explosive ways. We and the people toward whom our anger is directed suffer from it. Can something be done about anger?

A retreatant reported experiencing lots of energy during sittings, an energy that she felt was mostly generated by feeling angry about the sitting itself. Thoughts were running wildly about how she was wasting her time here while there was so much work left undone at home. "What should I do with all this energy?" she asked. "At times I feel like screaming! Is it all right to scream?"

We have all agreed to maintain outward silence during retreats. Screams are disturbing. If one really feels like screaming that's OK, but maybe one can find a ravine in the woods where it would not jar others. But it's an interesting question what to do about powerful energy surges like anger. My immediate response to the questioner was, "Let it be awareness! Awareness is boundless energy!"

Years ago a man came to see me before applying for retreat, asking if it would be all right if he expressed anger toward me during a meeting. I said it was all right. So he entered the meeting room one day with a tense, flushed face. Could he vent his anger right now, he asked. I nodded (not without inward trepidation!) and asked him, "Have you ever looked at anger directly?" No answer came—just a charged silence. We sat wordlessly for what seemed to be an eternity, and then he burst out laughing: "It doesn't have to be expressed!"

When a powerfully driven emotion gives way to simple awareness, it is like a miracle. What emerged from awareness wasn't screams and accusations but laughter and insight.

Psychological theories about what to do with anger abound and change with the times. I do not know if anger should be expressed or shouldn't be. The fact is that we do get angry, and it expresses itself instantly, verbally as well as nonverbally, throughout the body. So what is this anger? Can we go beyond the question, "What should I do with it?" and beyond answers like, "I should feel it in my body," or, "I should express it verbally or physically," or, "I ought to control it."

There is plenty to get in touch with when we're angry. Anger mobilizes the entire organism, mentally and physically—no single cell remains unaffected. Story lines run wildly, keeping the agitation going. Can we feel all these amazing physical and mental manifestations without resistance? If resistance is there, then can we feel it, look at it? Not try to shut it down by telling ourselves that it is dangerous to experience anger, or try to convince ourselves that we are wholly justified in what we are feeling? We really don't know. Every thought, every judgment about it intensifies confusion and agitation. Can simple awareness shed light and create a fresh, new space?

Can we trace anger as it is proceeding? Can we wonder innocently why I am getting angry? Not just get stuck with the immediate cause, but keep wondering: "What is under-neath that? Can it be illuminated with attention?" When we question it, observing it in the light of the question, what reveals itself is that we function in rigid patterns that do not want to be disturbed or interrupted. Memory structures in the brain and throughout the body about how we are, how things ought to be, what is right and what is wrong keep functioning fairly smoothly, but when they are interfered with, anger results.

These memory structures are wired into us from day one. Even an infant, who does not yet understand the spoken word, understands judgments conveyed by mother's and father's eyes and tone of voice. What does happen when we feel exploited, abused, humiliated, made fun of, or when we see it happening to others?

We have never learned a wise way to deal deeply with this because we are so used to either putting up with it, suffering from it, fighting it, or exploding over it. Either we continue darkly in our conditioned patterns, or there is an awakening of interest in what is going on for all of us, the abuser as well as the abused. This has nothing to do with sanctioning hurt-ful behavior, excusing it, or allowing it to continue.

Can we simply behold each other as we are from moment to moment? See ourselves, see everyone, as results of millen-nia-old conditioned patterns that have rigidly governed our behavior even though we don't want it to be so? Can we reach not just an intellectual understanding of this but direct insight into the power of our overwhelmingly strong condi-tioning? Then, maybe, we can begin to question things to-gether and communicate with each other in a new, intelligent, and compassionate way. Anger raging with its chemical tox-ins is not conducive to clearly examining and investigating the whole situation. On the contrary, it generates confusion in the mind.

What is needed is a fresh look into what is happening for all of us. Out of insight comes the energy to act in a clear way. This isn't easy by any means because we are so heavily conditioned in our patterns of reacting that we are not even cognizant of them most of the time. But that is not an immutable state of affairs. With a genuine curiosity there can be ever increasing awareness of how we react and how others react to us because of our reactions to them. We are all entangled together in a net of chain reactions. Bring them to light! Realize that when you talk to someone with an angry demeanor they are likely to respond in kind, triggering further irritation in you, and you in them, and on and on.

Most of us are scared of people who are angry, shouting, attacking, blaming. Out of fear, we respond angrily ourselves. It immediately touches memories of our childhood, years of helplessness and utter dependence on adults who often exploded in totally incomprehensible ways. Fear of angry people makes us not want to be near them—it is too upsetting, too intimidating. So, turning it around again, can we question, while we are angry, whether we are actually upsetting and intimidating other people? Maybe we don't really want to upset other people. A fresh moment of clarity and insight brings astonishing sensitivity and care.

As a child I was scared of my mother's anger, particularly when it was vented against my brother or the cook or nanny. I was deeply attached to all of them. My brother was often sullen, moody, obstinate, and did poorly in his schoolwork. I felt excruciating pain every time he was scolded, punished, or humiliated. Later, in my teens, I told my mother that I had been afraid of her anger all my life. It wasn't at all like me to talk to her like that, and she was visibly shocked. She didn't comprehend that I could have felt afraid and intimidated by her. It obviously did not fit the image she had of herself.

Memories now arise of times when I was not afraid of mother. We would sometimes go together into town to do shopping. Instead of taking the streetcar we walked the distance, and she would hold my hand, which made me feel wonderfully happy. Sometimes I would arrange my small hand in hers in a special way—all five fingers inside her hand—and she would go along with it happily. One time we were strolling through a department store, passing through narrow isles with merchandise arranged on tables left and right. I was too small to see the things on the tables but felt my mother's deep sadness, looking for something she couldn't find.

Can we have infinite patience with our own anger and the anger of others? Can our habitual reactions for or against someone be replaced with a wondering awareness that does not know? Can we try to understand each other on the deepest level, without images? We are the only laboratories for unfolding this understanding—anger wells up in all of us. Why? Not that it shouldn't, but just *why?* Let it reveal itself fully in present awareness without resistance.

12

Guilt and Responsibility

*T*HE GROUP DIALOGUE last night revolved around feelings of guilt and remorse for things we have done in the past that won't go away. Being tormented by guilt time and time again, we wonder if there is something we can do about it. Shall we look at this together? We all harbor guilt feelings that are frequently surfacing or hiding somewhere in the recesses of the mind.

The opening words of an aria from Bach's *St. Matthew Passion* come to mind: "Remorse and repentance tear the sinful heart asunder." The music is set in a minor key and is deeply moving. I loved singing it. Growing up under a political system and in a family where guilt feelings were surreptitiously cultivated, I learned to feel guilty early on. Feeling guilty is intimately connected with the fear of being found out, exposed, blamed or condemned, humiliated or punished. In a guilt-producing environment one becomes more tractable, ready to obey, eager to make up, willing to please and ingratiate oneself with one's parents or the people in power, all in an urge to ease the painful weight of fear and guilt. This fact is instinctively known and exploited by repressive governments, religious cults, and authoritarian teachers to create submissive followers. We are willing to subjugate ourselves to authority, turn over our possessions, and arouse superhuman energies demanded of us by the leader, all in an effort to assuage painful guilt feelings.

In my youth I was haunted by daily questions: "Did I do something wrong? Did I hurt someone? Is anyone angry with me? Could I be denounced to the Nazi authorities for what I said?" My sister and I would frequently commiserate about the burden of feeling "fiery coals heaped on our heads." Even today, at age seventy-two, the old unsettling question, "Did I say something wrong?" comes up in the mind. There is nothing wrong with that. What I said can be examined freshly anytime, and mistakes can be corrected. The mind need not keep returning to what has been seen and understood clearly.

Attending a Lutheran confirmation class at age fourteen, I was perplexed in hearing that Jesus, through his death on the cross, had taken the guilt of the world upon his shoulders. If this was so, why didn't I feel the guilt lifted from my shoulders? I asked the minister about this, and he showed consternation on his face, remained quiet, and went on to something else.

Much latter, in Zen training, the Roshi mentioned that the Sixth Patriarch Hui Neng had said something like this: "When others are wrong, I am wrong. When I am wrong, I alone am responsible." That statement puzzled me. What is the *I* that is wrong and the *I* that alone is responsible? What are the "others" who are wrong and not wrong? Later, in a moment of clarity, it struck me that "taking the sin of the world upon oneself," and "other people's wrongs being one's own wrongs" had the same quintessential meaning: In undivided presence without the separating feeling of self, there is only one world, one humanity, one indivisible life. The clouds drifting, birds flying, wind blowing, heart beating, breath flowing, and people people-ing are all right here without any barriers keeping us apart. Everything is here as it is, whole and complete, with no judge positioned outside of it. Just one amazing, ever changing, lovingly encompassing movement of life happening in empty space. The freedom of no one here!

When we become transparently aware of the inner commotion and conflicts caused by thoughts, emotions, and physical reactions, and at the same time the depth of stillness permeating everything, it dawns that what is happening in *me* is going on in everyone else. What you do, I am doing; what you have done, I have done. No one is doing it—everything is happening on its own in vast open space. The instant I condemn you, I've slipped back into the dualistic role of a judge confronting the guilty one. Judges always sit a few steps higher than the accused.

Does dying on the cross mean dying to the world of self-confinement, being indivisibly at one with sinner and saint? Atonement means *at-one-ment*. "My father, forgive them, for they know not what they are doing," was one of Jesus' last utterances. No word of judgment—just compassionate understanding of our hurtfully ignorant ways.

Is our sense of separation caused by self-consciousness at the root of our guilt feelings? Would we feel guilty if we fully realized our indivisibility? In our deluded state we are thoroughly convinced that "we" initiate things out of our own free will. We believe that we are at the controls of our behavior. We think that if we want our life to be different, we can choose to change it. If it doesn't change it is our own fault, or, even more likely, "other" people's fault. We assume that we know full well what we and others are doing.

Sitting quietly in silent retreats, we discover that we are

not in charge of events and the endlessly roaming thoughts with their bodily feelings, emotions, and reactions. We would love to turn off that constant stream of self-consciousness and rest for a while, but find *we* are incapable of doing it. We also notice that anger, hurt, greed, or fear arise instantly when our buttons are pushed, even though we may not want to react that way at all. We may resolve to respond differently next time, but find to our dismay that old entrenched programs have enormous power to keep repeating themselves against our will. Where is the freely willing *I* in all of this? Is there any freedom at all, or is it an illusion? Is the *I* real or is it an illusive story, a virtual reality? In observing our reactions and impulses, can we find the *me* doing these things, or is there just an ongoing process of thinking and doing things in accordance with deeply entrenched programs? The belief in an independent thinker and doer somewhere inside—is it all just convoluted *thinking?* Can we deeply wonder about this in quiet sitting and in our daily interactions with each other?

If we still feel strongly that "we" choose our actions—for example, to get up right now or to remain sitting—let's see if we can describe the whole process without needing to invoke this *I* at all. Listening inwardly, there are words like "I want to get up" and the action of getting up, or different words and actions: "I don't want to get up" and staying down. (It's more complex than this, but let's keep it as simple as possible.) Thoughts themselves trigger action or inaction. So why insist that there is a *me* driving thoughts and actions? Is it just because we have thought and talked like this for eons?

Frequently the question comes up that if we are not the doers of our actions, where is the place for taking responsibility? Aren't we responsible for our actions and their consequences? Again, can we look at it without assuming that a *me*-entity is needed to act responsibly?

Where do our actions come from? Can we look and listen together? When reactions arise out of the narrow, self-centered consciousness—the "virtual reality" in which we live most of the time—there is the thinking that *I* did something, and then taking blame and feeling guilty for what *I* did, or collecting praise and reward, with their good feelings and pride.

When the mind is uncluttered by self-conscious thoughts, the world is vast and open, permeated by an amazing intelligence and love. Right action happens in accord with the present situation, and there is no clinging to an image of oneself to be hurt or to feel proud. Things take place as one indivisible process—one's own reactions seen as an integral part of the whole picture. Painful or pleasurable sensations coming up are felt but need not be clung to. Clinging reveals itself as the narrowing of openness. Isn't that the essence of responsibility—responding in harmony with the present circumstances?

Coming back to Hui Neng's statement: "When others are wrong, I am wrong. When I am wrong, I alone am responsible." The first *I* is living in the delusive reality of the doer of deeds, the judge and the judged, the giver or the recipient of praise and blame. The other *I* is wholeness, seeing all and everything as wondrously interwoven in the fabric of infinite causes and effects, and yet no one here to feel "I did it," or "I didn't do it"! Freedom permeates it all.

One comes to a retreat to see if there can be some freeing from this incredible self-centered cocoon that separates us. It leaves no space to see the "others" and ourselves as we truly are. In our self-centered, programmed living all of us have done everything under the sun, both "good" and "bad."

There probably isn't any one of us who doesn't regret what we did in the past when we think of the harm and sorrow it caused other people. But can we also get a renewed clarity about it? We can watch this at the moment we are reacting angrily, feeling offended, and looking for reprisal. By watching it without identifying, we are learning about conditioned human beings, not just ourselves. In gaining insights into angry reactions as they arise, can we get a feel for how automatically programmed those reactions are? It's not *me* doing it! It comes out of the *me*-network, but it is not a deliberate choice.

We are watching very basic mechanisms. The Bible states "an eye for an eye, a tooth for a tooth": If you hurt me, I'll hurt you back. But while saying something hurtful to someone else out of anger or exasperation, we may also begin to hear ourselves more clearly, more compassionately—suddenly automatic impulses become more transparent. It is amazing. Some urge may come upon us to lash out angrily, but it is never too late for awareness to shed light. If there is stopping and listening attentively to what you are saying and what is going on in myself, space opens up in a wondrous way. You cannot hurt *me* if I am listening with energy that is not conditioned. Open listening has no *me*-center but wisdom and love.

I am not trying to make this into an ideal state for which we should strive—it can happen in an effortless way. If we strain, it becomes a *me*-movement, wanting to "have something," wanting to be better. One person said in a meeting today that for years he made enormous efforts to drop the conditioning, and now he sees it can't be done! He had tried the impossible! He felt a joyous relief from the habitual struggle to better himself. When this kind of insight happens, it is not at all depressing to see all the "stuff" going on. Discovery brings energy—the energy to be with what is here and not be torn asunder. At this moment there is no sinful heart. The heart is open—lovingly unfolding with this whole life, with all of its difficulties and joys. One does not have to be fighting oneself about something that one sees happening on its own.

When the memory comes up about what I have done wrong or what I should have done better, see that the mind need not become entangled in the impossible. It is clear that at the time I didn't know any better. Had there been insight, I would have acted differently. Clear presence now is being obscured by constantly thinking about what I did wrong in the past. In this fuzzy confusion the same old stuff keeps repeating itself. It takes wakefulness *now* in order not to repeat past patterns. Blind habit repeats and repeats. Clear seeing throws light on habits, revealing their fragmenting ways.

We are not fragments—we are the whole. This is not an idea—it is so. When useless things don't hang in the mind . . . listen . . . the crows . . . just *caw, caw, caw, caw!*

13

The Trace of Attachment

*I*N WATCHING ONE'S DEEP YEARNING at a time of great loss to get back what once gave joy and happiness, it is clear that such yearning is not merely a mental process. It's a palpable physical movement involving one's entire bodymind so powerfully that it could be called an addiction—the addiction to relive and reexperience the joyful moments of one's past. The brain is very cooperative and resourceful in this endeavor, creating colorful "videos" of bygone pleasures and keeping them running while triggering actual physical sensations of enjoyment. Sometimes it feels as though the delights created by fantasy play even surpass what was actually experienced before.

This is an incredibly compelling process, not only repeating through memories what has given pleasure and security in the past, but also projecting past painful events and evoking ache, distress, and fear in the present. In my personal case of having just lost my beloved husband, the vivid memories of joyfully sharing our life together relentlessly activate the convulsions of a grieving heart.

So is it possible to experience anything presently without its immediately leaving a memory trace in the brain that demands repetition with its pain and pleasure? Is it possible to behold anything without instantly creating attachment?

Many religions teach that enjoyment is not the problem, only attachment is. Don't be or become attached to anything or anyone, if you want to escape suffering. Well, this is easier said than done. One witnesses clearly how the brain is deeply programmed to record as memory every instant of one's life, not only the actual occurrence of the moment, but all the sensations, feelings, and emotions connected with it. Remembrances are intricately connected with each other so that almost any associated thought, sound, sight, smell, taste, or touch sets off happy or sad feelings. So is it humanly possible to behold anything without automatically creating attachment and the compelling drive to repeat?

I don't know. Recording our experiences is a crucial function of the brain in order to remember what has worked out well (in terms of pleasure) and what has brought on danger and pain. We probably would not have survived without it. That the bodymind desires pleasure and tries to avoid pain is a plain fact within the immediate experience of all of us.

Can anything be done to change that? Can the programmed recording of the brain go into abeyance so that attachment to memories does not come into being? (Krishnamurti used to ask a similar question many times, almost demanding that the brain stop registering.)

What is not effective is beating oneself for being attached or for not being able to drop attachment. Believing that I could stop being attached if I only had the right willpower or discipline to abstain just causes guilt feelings but does not bring understanding. Can one rather question and observe carefully what is actually going on in one's daily life and wonder if it is humanly possible *not* to become attached to experiences in this moment of aliveness? There is so much beauty around and a lot of tenderness and affection among human beings. Is it possible to behold beauty—the sparkling, color-soaked ocean sands at low tide as the sun is setting and the moon is rising, or touching each other's hearts lovingly— without this becoming the seed for future longing and the pain of loss and grief? In the aliveness of this moment, can the brain remain quiescent without the stir of wanting, with its habitual drives in simple abeyance? Such a moment does not create yearning for more. It is without time.

We do not need to shun beauty because "I don't want to get attached to it," nor to avoid relationship because "I don't want to be attached and then suffer the pain of loss." Such schemes atrophy the heart. Rather, can we wonder whether for moments at a time we can live so fully, so unencumbered by self-reference, that no traces remain in the brain that demand repetition?

It's for each of us to wonder and maybe come upon. It cannot be taught or practiced.

And when the other happens as it does, finding ourselves caught up in attachment with its sorrow, grief, and yearning, how do we look and listen in the midst of it? Can the mind, in looking and questioning, see through the veil of resistance, letting pain and pleasure be what they are and leaving them to do what they will without interfering? Not needing to control or get rid of what is there, just beholding it vastly. Not the command "You must" or "You must not," but simple presence, which is innocent. Wondering without knowing.

14

What Is My Innermost Core?

Someone mentioned in a meeting that he used to work very hard at being aware and mindful—that it was an exhausting effort. And then, suddenly, out of nowhere, undivided presence is dawning on its own without needing to be forced at all! Unexpectedly, whatever is happening is revealed in effortless awareness. Is this our true being—an alive presence, undivided, without effort or conflict?

The words we use to describe this do not matter. Use the word that you find most meaningful and intimate. Sometimes we just say *listening, breathing, chirping, raining, awaring.* Simply being here is all! Not as a "somebody"—a successful meditator or a poor one, for all that is thought, continuously separating and dividing.

Can thoughts of being someone important, or unimportant, become transparent in awareness, thoughts about doing well or doing poorly? The brain is in the business of constantly creating or maintaining self-identities: "I am this which is good" or "I am that which is bad." Along with these identities go ever changing energies throughout the body, depending on how we happen to think about ourselves at this moment. Thinking I am good brings pleasant sensations; thinking I am bad results in turmoil. Can the immediate connection between self-judgments and physical sensations come into clear awareness? To see it as an automatic happening without anybody *doing* it! We believe that *we* are in control, but where is the controller in these instant connections between thought and emotion?

How quiet, how simple, can present listening be? Regardless of whether there is inner stillness or noisy agitation, can wholesome listening be quiet? Getting quieter and quieter means less and less resistance to what is here, fewer judgments, less opposition, less fighting. Quietness is letting everything appear in awareness as it is, whether it be fantasy, planning for the future, or worrying about the past, whether it is pain or pleasure, or an unexpected clearing of the mind.

The powerful urge to know what is going on, and instantly reacting to that knowledge, judging it good or bad, are ingrained functions of the brain. We are talking about the mental activity to recognize and verbalize internally whatever is being experienced from moment to moment, such as saying to oneself, "I'm having an easy time," "I'm having a terribly hard time," or "I will never get it," and then reacting to these evaluations mentally and physically. From age-old habit we seem to feel at home in what we think is going on, instantly reacting to the ongoing story line, whether it is accurate or not. We rarely doubt our words about ourselves. We know the words and are not used to questioning them.

Is it all right not to know? I mean right here in sitting together quietly. (I'm not talking about knowing how to cook dinner or what plants to pull out in weeding the garden.) Is it all right to live for a moment without seeking for a description, an explanation, a comment? This bodymind is addicted to its explanations—they provide the pseudo-safety and security of the known.

Being here right now, is it all right not to know what I am all about—what I am, where I am going, how I am feeling? What am I without thinking about myself, without words and pictures, without identities? It is an indescribable relief to realize that I don't have to know anything about myself, this moment of being here, quietly!

Whatever is going on is going on by itself. The brain functions according to its ongoing programs, recognizing, naming, associating, comparing, interpreting, reacting. There is no *me* doing it—it just happens. Can this become transparently clear in choiceless awareness?

Now there is just listening and wondering whether thinking about myself has to continue this moment of just being. No need to say that thinking about myself *shouldn't* take place. When it's going on, it's going on, consciously or unconsciously. Right now, there is hearing the words and listening openly in between the words. Just the listening, stillness, now. Do we need to *know* what anything is?

The darkness of not knowing is prior to knowledge. It is being before knowing. Whatever is taking place habitually, can it simply come and go in nonjudging awareness?

It is an amazing discovery: the less we know, the fresher everything looks! When we think we know the flower we don't really look at it—the mind is caught up in the false certainty that it knows daisies and therefore can't behold the wonder of that little white-petaled flower with a bright yellow dot inside. The knowing brain just sees the image of a daisy.

The other day I washed the oatmeal pot and, thinking it was clean, put it on the rack to dry. Later, picking it up again, I noticed dried oatmeal stuck on the side. Why hadn't I seen it while washing the pot? I *thought* it was clean!

Someone asked, "Why does this *me*-ness, this self-centered feeling, arise when we realize that it causes such a painful sense of separation? How did it ever start in the first place?"

I don't know how the *me* started in the first place—maybe there isn't any "first place." But all of us can watch *me*-ness as it is arising from moment to moment. We can find out about it if we are really deeply interested and curious. But our concerns wax and wane—the more gratifying the ways of ego, the less concern about it; but with renewed suffering the interest returns.

We often talk about getting angry when our personal ways are thwarted by someone, getting vindictive at being criticized, or being tormented when slighted by others. What is it that is being defended and protected? Can we ask this question freshly as hurt is felt anew and defensiveness springs into action? We all suffer from this, and yet it seems so difficult to remain attentive from beginning to end. Time and again we feel isolated, ignored, insulted, or rejected, and strangely justified in feeling that way. What gets hurt, what feels isolated and rejected?

Can we start with not knowing the answer? Not just say, "It is my ego that got hurt." That's talking from *knowing*, isn't it? We know lots of psychological stuff about "the ego," but whatever is actually happening while being criticized or being told off needs to reveal itself directly as buttons get pushed. Can we examine this, not for the purpose of getting rid of ego hurt, but rather to witness ourselves in live action?

This means attending openly as we get upset, irritated, or anxious in retreat as well as in daily life. As one tries to get to the innermost core of it all, it cannot be found. All one comes upon is a complex networking of ideas, images, and memories hooking into disturbing sensations and emotions that cry out in pain and anger and seek protection. Is there any innermost core beyond all this?

Again, can we start out by not knowing? Can we inquire out of the darkness of not knowing? Into the darkness of not knowing? Inquiring does not mean repeating a question. Questioning here means, "I truly don't know. All I know is what I remember from the past, from reading, or from hearing what other people have said." What is the innermost core of myself, right now?

Silent wondering is facing a question that cannot be answered. All that comes to the searching brain is what it already knows—ideas about a soul, concepts of the spark of god within me, belief in a divine essence, the atman, a Buddha in my belly, or whatever. Right now I don't even know whether there is such a thing as "within," or an "innermost core"—those too are seen to be concepts! Can there be quiet wondering, listening, bare of any ideas?

The space of listening without knowing is open, unoccupied, undivided by thought. There are birds twittering, a fan is humming, people are breathing, coughing—a palpitating energy not confined within the skin. No one is separate from all this, nothing needs to be shut out or shut in. No inside and no outside here! One vibrant aliveness without boundaries, an embrace of love.

15

What Is It That Dies?

A LETTER TO TONI AND HER RESPONSE

Toni,

A few nights ago I was watching a TV documentary on African wildlife. In one of the scenes a water buffalo had accidentally fallen into a mud bog. The narrator said that the animal was stuck there and couldn't extricate itself. A pride of hungry lions spied the creature and began to sniff at it. At first they weren't sure what to do with prey that didn't run from them. Finally, one of the lions began to chew on the water buffalo's tail. The poor animal began to writhe and wail. The lions then began to literally eat the animal alive as the camera rolled.

What is the meaning of suffering? Why does any kind of pain even exist? Please don't tell me that it's all just thought. I realize you can't give me some magical answer or cure for suffering, but if you could just point in the direction to look for an answer it would perhaps help.

Three years ago my father died of cancer. I was by his

side at the moment of death and much of the time several days before. He was an agnostic nearly his whole life—a very rational, scientific-minded man. A couple of days before he died, he began to experience dreams or visions of hell. He turned to me with a fearful, pained look upon his face and said: "I've been to hell. It was horrible . . . I kept falling and falling and there was no bottom." Another time he said he had lost us (myself and my brother) in "air-traffic control." He seemed to be going through a sort of purgatory those last few days. He seemed to be experiencing a lot of psychological pain and fear along with the physical agony. A few hours before he died he finally became quieter. He had gone into a sort of coma from pneumonia. I stood by his side, holding his hand and listening to his labored breathing. I leaned close to his ear and told him that it was OK, he didn't have to struggle anymore, that he could rest, that he could go now. At that very instant he took a deep breath and exhaled completely. That was all—he was dead. Do the visions he had mean anything? If so, what?

There are questions that have been in my mind for several years: "What is it that lives and dies?" and "Where do you go upon death?" When Dad died, one of the children asked, "Where did he go, Daddy?" If one does not start out with any preconceived beliefs or conclusions, this is a natural thing to ask. It seems the very question is wrong somehow—similar to watching a horse running on TV, and when someone turns the television off you ask where the horse went. Going and coming? There's really no way to answer that question because its very premise is wrong. Still, even though it's the wrong question, Toni, what *is* it that lives and dies?

Dear ———,

Let's start with your first question: "What is the meaning of suffering? Why does any kind of pain even exist? Please don't tell me that it's all just thought."

The writhing, wailing water buffalo is not thinking—he is crying out with pain, as any sentient living being with a nervous system and sensitive organs would naturally do. Rocks do not thrash about and scream when cut or crushed—they do not manifest the same sensitive aliveness that animals, humans, and plants do.

Are you asking whether it is possible to be alive and yet not experience pain and hurt? Does your question imply that aliveness should be without sensitivity of pain in order to be meaningful? That there is something wrong with experiencing pain?

Don't we ache physically *because* we are alive? Could we ever feel joy, pleasure, beauty, and love without being equally vulnerable to the aches and pains of a sensitive, tender body?

You mention that you don't expect a magical answer to cure suffering, but would like a pointer for looking. So let's look together. Can we see that experiencing physical pain as well as pleasure is inseparably woven into the delicate fabric of living? Sensitivity and vulnerability are not selective.

Now—is suffering the same thing as experiencing physical pain? You were watching a TV documentary and saw the agony of a water buffalo trapped in a bog and eaten alive by lions. More than that—you may have felt pain and horror in your own heart and guts. Pain is not merely produced through tangible physical impact—it can be evoked by thought, memory, and image. We feel pain when remembering hurt, and we ache when seeing or hearing about the pain of others.

And we feel additional torture by reacting to physical pain with thoughts like, "Why is life so full of pain? It's senseless and cruel. I hate it. It's unjust. I wish it were different!"

Such thinking causes extra pain that one could call suffering. Thought not only evokes agitation, doubts, self-pity, and pity for others, but it also creates the idea or image of the sufferer, the victim. The instant I think of myself or another as a suffering victim, it's already become suffering! Reacting against physical hardship in words and images causes acute suffering, which is different from the pure experiencing of physical pain. Are we together in this? Can we investigate this the next time there is physical pain, wondering whether it can be felt directly, nonjudgmentally, without a story line picking it up and converting it into "my terrible suffering?" This takes great gathering of energy in awareness.

Does your question "What is the meaning of suffering?" imply that you are questioning why sentient beings cause each other endless pain and suffering? Religious teachers throughout the ages have taught that suffering is necessary for spiritual growth and deliverance. Is that so?

I can see no deliverance in suffering itself. Just a moment ago we looked at the birth of suffering as the intellect takes over, weaving words and picture stories around the occurrence of pain, creating the sufferer and thus intensifying and solidifying the agony. We also asked what happens when painful experience is unconditionally met in an innocent way. Could *that* be the ending of suffering? Can we experiment with this directly as pain arises and ideas are seen weaving around and about the pain? What happens as the story weaving becomes more and more transparent in awareness?

Right now I'm wondering—was the water buffalo completely present in his agonizing death throes? No thinking like humans do about past, present, and future, about justice and injustice, meaning or absence of meaning in living and dying. Just the pain, the thrashing and groaning as life is struggling, painfully ending, and simultaneously feeding life. Are the devourer and the devoured separate in the whole thing?

As we watch the seemingly absurd cruelty of life, inflicted by life upon itself, the question "What is the meaning of it all?" becomes a profound one to ponder. Will one wonder deeply while leaving it alone at the same time—not expecting theories, opinions, or beliefs for answers? Can a question be held in the darkness of not knowing?

You are asking whether the visions your father had before his last exhalation mean anything. Who is to say? We all are manifestations of an ever accumulating and self-expressing consciousness that includes visions of heaven and hell floating through our waking, sleeping, and dreaming states like clouds in the sky. Is one caught up in the clouds, or can there be direct insight into their true nature?

Insight is not a vision—it reveals ever changing mind formations coming and going in vast limitless space without time.

"What is it that lives and dies?" you ask, and, "Where do you go upon death?"

Yesterday, as I walked up the hill, some shriveled flowers lined the path—an early frost had snuffed out their delicate lights. Other hardier plants were blooming during the warming day. Your question came to mind: "What *is* it that lives and dies?" We usually ask this question when someone close to us dies or when we ponder our own death. Rarely do we want to know what it is in a flower that has died. We take it for granted that the earth displays constantly appearing, changing, and disappearing colors, forms, and textures.

A moment ago, there was a loud thud against the window. I looked out and saw a beautiful bird lying quietly on the patio, eyes half-open, the white dappled belly and yellow tail feathers freely exposed. The body was still warm but without the lively motion that ended in a crash and fall.

What is it that died? What is it that is born? A bird has died, another one has hatched, an old man has exhaled his last breath, a baby has left the womb, a flower has frozen as another one opened its purple petals. What is it that is born and dies?

Once, when I was a child, I looked into a baby buggy passing by and saw a tiny head with two big eyes peeking out from under the covers. The thought occurred right then: "That could be *me* looking out at the world! Every time there is a new baby, that could be *me*! How would I ever know that it wasn't *me*?" That thought brought joy—absence of fear.

Toward the end of your letter you feel that the question "What is it that lives and dies?" is wrong somehow. It's like asking "Where did the horse go?" after turning off the TV show. Our whole life may be nothing but a continuous show—the same, different, old, and new play—on and off all the time! When it's on we live, love, and suffer—when it's off, the vastness is dark and silent and doesn't know about birth and death.

Can there be a moment of stillness without knowing?

PART THREE

Relationship

16

Can There Be Personal Freedom in a Committed Relationship?

*I*T'S A BRIGHT WINTER MORNING—sunshine flooding through the windows and doors, warming the hands and face.

Now some clouds appear—everything is darkening. Then the sun appears again, brightening the world.

Last night someone said, "Toni, you have talked about how close you were with Kyle, how you shared just about everything—the joy of that sharing, the love of it, and the pain of grief when it was all gone." Yes, the painful longing for a lost person surges instantly when the memory arises. The bodymind is deeply attuned to its past pleasures, good times, and loving feelings and wants them to last forever. This happens automatically without any conscious intention. It's not just a mental but also a physical longing to repeat what was beautiful, enjoyable, and so intimately customary.

The questioner continued, "On the one hand, I yearn to share the beauty and joy as well as the difficulty and pain that comes with living together, but on the other hand, I dread the loss of my personal freedom."

What freedom?

The questioner had recently gotten married, but this question is frequently raised by people who have been married for a while, or those who are about to set up living together: What will happen to my cherished personal freedom?

In living together there is not just the happiness of sharing good times but also the relentless demand to share the tiring chores of the household and the tribulations of difficult times together. Neither person carries the inevitable burdens alone. Where is my "personal freedom" in this way of shared living?

It takes genuine interest and alertness to ask this question, particularly during difficult times. Emotionally charged story lines about my difficult fate spin out quickly in this ever active brain: "I've lost my precious freedom; I can't do what I want to anymore; my needs are left unfulfilled; I'm too restricted; I have no time for myself; I'm just doing things for others." Along with the spinning out of such assertions come conflicting emotions and physical tensions. There may be something to these assessments, but do they accurately reflect the total situation of which we are an integral part? Is there any room left in the discontented, frustrated mind to take in more than its own sad lot?

Of course, we all have needs and must take care of them adequately—the need for nourishing food, for rest, exercise, fresh air, fun and laughter, and some quiet time. But I learned during Kyle's declining years how little we actually need—how the smallest of joys and a bit of respite here and there went a long way to refresh the exhausted bodymind as long as the deep affection between us was alive and its source remained unobstructed. When the mind is alert and present it need not be taken over by narratives about "how badly off I am." No need to get trapped in the pit of self-pity once that danger is clearly understood.

So what is this "personal freedom" that we treasure so much and want to preserve no matter what? At the same time, we also want to live together intimately, have sex, enjoy good companionship, take trips together, share work, acquire a house, a yard, furniture, computers, raise children, and so on. All that—but also maintain our "personal freedom"! Can there be clarity about what is actually workable and what is a dream?

We haven't really gone into what is freedom. Is *that* the dream—thinking that freedom is being able to do what I want whenever I want to do it? Is doing what I want to do true freedom? We *think* it is. I want to be free to do what I want and let nothing interfere with that. But that scheme never works, no matter whether we live alone or together, because there is always something we want but cannot do. There is always something that interferes. The "freedom" to do what I want is chained inextricably to the dream of a separate self.

Is there any freedom that is not a dream?

I remember years ago reading in a book by D. T. Suzuki a Zen teacher's statement that "freedom is the elbow not bending outward." What an amazing statement! The elbow is unable to bend outward—at a certain point it comes to a full stop. How can it be freedom not to bend beyond its limitation? To the rational mind it seems incomprehensible that restriction could be freedom. It thinks of freedom as the absence of restriction! But the logical intellect is not all there is to profound understanding. Can presence with its spacious awareness replace our customary resistance to being at one with restriction no matter how unbearable it may seem? *Being at one* seems quite a cliché these days—almost every spiritual tradition teaches us "to become one" with our problems. What does it really mean, being at one?

It is an unhurried, undivided presence in which the in-grained, obsessive scanning for the next better thing becomes clearly transparent and ceases to agitate. It is being here com-pletely in all simplicity, attentive to the amazing detail of the moment that is usually slurred over in the restlessness of discontent. In simple presence with what is here right now, be it joyful or painful, an amazing freedom reveals itself. It cannot be described or explained in words. It is the elbow not bending outward—the freedom to be totally, effortlessly the way things are at this moment. No straining to get around the work at hand, no fighting it, bargaining with it, complaining about it, or suffering from it. No story line spinning out to create me, the victim. If the story does start spinning, can it be seen quickly and abandoned just like step-ping out of a poison ivy patch the moment we recognize it?

When wanting and fearing aren't restricting the view, there is the freedom to love. It is not asking for things in return. Asking for things in return is our customary way of relating to each other. It may be practical and helpful in living together: I do this for you, you do that for me, we do things for each other in an equal way. But if you don't or cannot do things for me anymore (as in the case of disabil-ity), then what takes place? Are frustration, resentment, and self-pity stirring? Do these movements arise from the situa-tion itself or from the *story* I use to describe it to myself in plaintive terms? It happens very quickly to all of us and needs to be seen and understood intelligently lest it quickly dims the light of affection. Sometimes just being with someone who is not brimful of ego, who is not asking for things for him- or herself, opens up that wellspring of love. Kyle's amazing way of being at one with his ever deteriorating body evoked love in everybody near him. In his presence there was space for everybody.

Right now, reading all this, does the desire arise to get this loving openness? Or to get rid of the self center? There is no way of getting rid of self-centered thinking. All of us are deeply programmed in the ways of wanting and getting and fearing for ourselves. These movements of thought need to be detected as they are occurring and as they have occurred in the past—learning firsthand that *they* are our lack of freedom. Not solely understanding this intellectually but experiencing directly the coming and going of inner contraction when the story is running. Awareness is always here. It may be hidden, like the sun behind the clouds, but it can shine forth instantly in a marvelous way, shedding light on our conditioned ways—our suffering. No need to get rid of it. Let awaring do its own wondrous thing.

Somebody asked, "Does relationship help in this?"

Yes, it does. Relationship is a living mirror if we are willing to look into it and learn as we go. In our cocoon existence, largely oblivious of how we are affecting others, we only think about how other people are affecting *us*. But when the cocoon opens, there is a growing awareness about how we are affecting others with our moods, gestures, and words. Not that "we shouldn't," but witnessing each other directly, with growing space. Can we actually let somebody tell us how we have affected them without getting hurt and immediately scrambling for cover? How are we affecting each other? Is it a living question? Not just insisting that I need the freedom to express my feelings. That's all right if the openness to communicate works both ways. But often we are afraid of hearing others tell us how we are affecting them. For candid and compassionate communicating to work well, there has to be mutuality. Mutual affection. Absence of hostility. A quiet listening space that lies deeper than the superficial hurt or defense that springs from our conditioned programs. Do I really need defending myself to feel secure? What needs to be defended, what needs to be secure?

So next time I notice that I am defending myself, can I stop, look, and listen? Can I ask, "What is going on? Why am I doing this?" Listen deeply. What is there to defend?

Can there be the insight that there is nothing to defend? No one there! Just images and stories with their bodily sensations! The freedom to see that!

17

Judging Others

*L*ET'S LOOK SOME MORE into this whole matter of judgment. Someone said that when they first heard a talk about listening and looking without judging, there was a happy feeling that maybe there could be an altogether different way of being—a genuine release from constantly evaluating oneself and others. But, in coming to more talks and meetings, this person was beginning to experience increasing judgments about their judgments! Is there any way out? Let's look at it freshly.

Let's see if it is possible to behold judging without judging. Right now, as raindrops are splattering on leaves, roof, and windows, can the listening and looking free itself of thinking complications, allowing whatever is there to appear, unfold, and disappear without any need to interfere? Judgment comes and goes; the judgment of judgment appears and disappears. No need to hold on to anything in the mind. Nothing stays forever, not even rocks. Rocks eroded by water end up as sand. And what is sand? A universe of particles moving in empty space!

At times if feels as though there is a solid rock wall inside, separating us from ourselves and from each other. We may think this is a true state of affairs, but nothing stays the same for even one single instant. Rocklike ideas about *me* and *you* and *the world* have a tenacious longevity, but in an instant their transparent emptiness can be seen. Emptiness means no one there to judge, nothing to be grasped or rejected.

Can we just be quietly aware of this movement of judgment, the constant criticism of self and others, without any need to do anything about it—just being here spaciously with whatever is happening without needing to change or work at understanding it? Understanding comes entirely on its own.

Someone told me that, while sitting, the ever critical state of mind suddenly disappeared. It was gone. What was left was utter amazement and joy. Without doing anything, fog dissipates.

One of the by-products of criticizing others is making oneself feel important as someone who knows what is right. We crave the security of feeling superior, of being in the know. Even knowing that I am not as good as others can become an identity to be clung to and insisted upon. It all revolves around this *me* thing—*me* this and *me* that. In truth the *me* is *no*-thing other than thought, memory, and sensations that happen to have tremendous electrochemical power within this bodymind, giving it the false impression of existing as a separate entity among other separate entities.

One question that often comes up is, Can we live our life in social relations without judgments? Aren't there things that need to be judged right or wrong in order to live together in an orderly, sane, and safe manner? Aren't cruelty, violence, and destructiveness truly evil, demanding judgment and condemnation?

We are not talking here about the social conventions of behavior that exist in any organized group of people with their standards, judgments of transgressions, and sanctions. Here I am interested in questioning what makes for transgressions rather than judging and condemning them out of a socially conditioned mind-set.

I avoid the word "evil." It instantly triggers deeply conditioned reactions like revulsion, or sanctimoniousness, obscuring clarity about what is really happening. Rather than labeling and judging, can we understand deeply, thoroughly, what is going on within ourselves and in our relationships with each other? Can we grasp directly the whole process of violence and its inevitable consequences?

We may find that we can be so entranced with our ingrained ideas, so entrenched in our collective convictions about who is good and who is evil, that ideas like "Jews are a subhuman race," "Muslims are terrorists," "gays are neurotics," easily turn into reactions of blind hatred and collective rage: the obsession to hurt, punish, or annihilate the "enemy."

So—in thinking about someone's "wrongdoing," are we being in a judgmental mood, blindly, stubbornly identified with a position from which we condemn or accept? Or are we in an open, impartial space of wondering and examining what is going on in ourselves, and why anyone would be doing what they are doing?

Suspending the judgment of someone else's violent action, we may discover, maybe to our surprise, a movement of animosity and violence in ourselves. Can we examine it thoroughly, not looking away, not needing to condemn? Don't actions of violence and animosity speak clearly for themselves, revealing their driving ignorance, their divisiveness and destructiveness—their lack of love? In our relationships with each other, do we need judgment and condemnation, or rather understanding and compassion?

This is the miracle of awareness: it gives birth to intelligent and compassionate action. Awareness does not judge, condemn, or accept, because it has no *me*-ness to be defended or nurtured. In the wonder of clear seeing, *me*-ness is in abeyance, leaving infinite room for love.

18

The Importance of Communicating

LET'S TALK ABOUT the great difficulty we have in communicating freely with each other—a topic that comes up frequently in meetings, both individual and group. As we hear each other talk, as we speak to someone or are confronted ourselves with sensitive topics, instantaneous reactions are triggered throughout the bodymind, creating a smog of confusion and upset. Neurochemical charges excite the organs, mobilize the glands, stiffen the muscles, cause the head to throb, and constrict or even close down the senses. Anger, hurt, sadness, the frustration of not being heard and understood—these feelings instantly express themselves physically, playing havoc with quiet listening, clear thinking, and free communicating.

Each of us brings to an encounter layers and layers of conditioned habits and mind-sets that heavily cloud our perceptions of each other. Most of the time we're not even aware of our inability to really hear or see what someone else is saying. Nor are we fully aware of what we ourselves are saying and how it affects others. We meet each other, or rather *don't* meet each other, because we are overflowing with our own preconceptions.

Is it possible to perceive accurately at this moment what we are all about? Can a viable openness unfold as we are communicating right now, making visible, audible, what separates us?

It's impossible to hear ourselves and each other accurately unless there is some sustained awareness that sheds light on the physical and mental interference that operates in us all from moment to moment. In the felt absence of clarity, can we go easy on interpreting and remembering "for sure" what we said or what someone else has said, not insisting on the accuracy of our perceptions? Most of the time we feel certain that we know and remember correctly what happened during our discussions. But do we really? If there was no clear perception at that moment, can there possibly be accurate memory now? How can we tell with certainty what we are saying to each other and how we are saying it while the heart is pounding, the blood is rushing to the head, the throat feels constricted, and muscle fibers spring into action?

It may be helpful to get back together after an argument at a more quiet time and wonder, "What did we really mean when we said such and such a thing? Did we really say it the way we remember it right now?"—not expecting that such questioning will necessarily get at the truth of what really went on, because the brain records what enters through the filter of preconceptions.

Also, we resist admitting having said something that doesn't look or sound good right now. We feel guilty about past behavior that doesn't go along with our idealized image of ourselves—an image to which we cling for dear life. So we say, "You misunderstood me. I didn't say that at all."

We may not be able to clear up what happened yesterday or many years ago, unless both of us are fairly free from grasping images about ourselves right now. For this freedom to come into being, our self-imagery—with its need to be propped up or defended, and the problematical confinement this produces—has to become transparent. Becoming transparent to ourselves and to each other, without the interference of any kind of cover-up, seems to be one of the most difficult things in human relationship. We anxiously resist being confronted with the truth of our own moment-to-moment "ugly" reactions. Instead we cling to ideas of how we should look and sound, and how the "others" should be, a clinging that results in misunderstanding after misunderstanding—the aching lack of affectionate relationship. True relationship between you and me is the spontaneous suspension of all imagery about me and you—the unencumbered clarity of what is happening right now. Otherwise we inevitably get confused and hurt.

Hurts are remembered years after the actual incident took place. The memory of these hurts mobilizes the same feelings of humiliation, anger, frustration, or sadness that were experienced the first time. Nothing has happened right now except the arousal of a fleeting memory, yet the bodymind is flooded with painful emotions pressing for all kinds of verbal and physical release. How utterly amazing we are!

Will we question and look this time at what is getting hurt as we feel hurt? Do we feel compelled to understand clearly this ever repeating event, which has been recycling throughout human history with grave consequences? Or is the overriding thrust of our conditioning the need to blame someone—else: "You did it to me. It's your fault. I'll never forget this as long as I live. You'll have to pay for this. I demand an apology." There's nothing wrong with apologizing. But does it clarify what it is that gets hurt, or does it instead reinforce images about you and me?

It's good to bring unresolved things up and question them

together, not in isolation, because without direct and careful communication together, image production thrives. In the absence of direct, clarifying contact with each other, the brain keeps elaborating the mental stories about what happened between you and me, keeping itself excited and entertained by its own emotion-arousing narration.

It's strange that it should be so difficult to understand each other, since every one of us is fundamentally made of the same stuff, the same star dust, the same elements combining in each human body. We're told that we all consist of more than 80 percent water. Like the oceans. The trillions of molecules, atoms, electrons, and ever tinier particles and waves are the same in you and me, in everyone, in the trees and flowers, earth and water. The same intergalactic space permeates each atom of material substance—electrons and particles skipping around in empty space. We're not really water molecules; we're mostly empty space filled with energy! You and I—all of us—space and energy, with an astounding potential to create, adapt, and disappear.

All of us had the same evolutionary history, each one of us has temporarily emerged from the same vast pool of genetic material contained in each tiny egg and sperm. Without food none of us survives, without oxygen and water we die. All of us. Every living thing. It's the same for you and me, whether we're here now or whether we were here millions of years ago.

Moreover, all of us are similarly conditioned to think and talk as those around us think and talk. We may believe that we talk and think uniquely, but where do our unique thoughts come from? Where does the thought of *I* and *you* come from? Can we wonder quietly without immediately trying to know?

All of us human beings are caught in the process of identification, believing that we truly are what our various beliefs tell us we are—believing that we are our names, our bodies, our self-images, our ideas about gender, family, social status, religion, nationality, job, possessions. Maybe not necessarily identifying with the image of *me* as the freewheeling separate individual (which happens to be such an important concept in our Western world), but instead identifying with the group to which we belong. These identifications powerfully mold, shape, and divide human beings whether we live here or at the other end of the world, today or millennia ago.

We all have different ideas about "what I am," "what you are," what the world is, what is right, good or bad, holy or profane, and these ideas masquerade for the truth—we don't see that they are all just tentative assumptions. Also, there usually is an unquestioned attachment to our views. Attachments go together with a firm defense system holding them in place. To keep feeling secure we feel compelled to remain anchored in what we believe we are. But what are we really?

Can we question all this thoroughly, and experience directly the attachment to our ideas about ourselves? Can we immediately feel the defenses that spring into action when these beliefs are threatened? One may be struck with awe by the power of our identifications!

Here is an example: We may become identified with a little marble in playing a board game. You know that game where you can kick another marble off the board when you land on its space, or get kicked off yourself? As you play, you *become* the marble, getting hurt when you're kicked off and retaliating gleefully when you can kick off someone else. All of oneself a tiny marble with memory and feelings!

In meeting together with all of our different backgrounds and conditionings, our varying beliefs and ideas, our commonly shared self-righteousness and defensiveness—can we wonder if it is possible to listen to each other in a totally fresh way? Can we listen to an angry person without immediately taking it personally—not becoming angry and defensive ourselves? Or maybe see the personal reactions coming up and simply watching them dispassionately? I don't mean *thinking* about them, but rather *seeing* the whole body be affected and how we've already missed what someone just said because our head was buzzing with reaction—feeling wronged or needing to right something. I may find that I do not want people to be the way they are. I want them to be the way I want them to be. And I watch too the constant discontent with myself. I want to be different—I would like to be able to listen freely, to be open without encumbrance. And yet I don't seem to be able to bring it off through willpower. There seems to be a deep fear holding me back, a resistance to look at what it is I'm holding on to. What is that?

Can there be a moment of stillness without any knowing?

It is so difficult to listen freely while I'm holding on to self-images. "I'm right. I need to win. I can't afford to be wrong." It may not even be verbal. Can one feel this holding on and question it? Not forcing to drop it. Dropping happens on its own. Dropping comes out of wisdom, the wisdom of simply being what is given, unadulterated. Seeing ourselves and our preferences, our tendencies, and the almost impossible difficulty of taking someone precisely as he or she is.

Is this possible?

Of course it is! It's all we've got anyway. All we have is each other as we are from now to now to now, in an open communal exploration, in which all our compulsions to change each other are freely questioned and exposed. Then rigid things begin to loosen. The defense systems may begin to dismantle on their own. When we're delving together into common human problems, no one is being attacked—we're all alike under investigation! Self-defense is not needed here—it gets in the way. This becomes transparent, and *that's* the change.

No one can directly see for someone else. It has to happen here, and here, and here, for each person, spontaneously. And it actually does, doesn't it? Maybe just for an instant! Many people bemoan the fact that insight is so fleeting, so quickly fogged over with old, habitual patterns. "What's the use of having momentary insight," we ask, "when it's so quickly gone again?" One realizes one's complete helplessness in bringing it about or in keeping it. That's the beginning of wisdom!

For one moment, can we leave everyone and everything unchanged just the way it is? Here we are all together—one complete movement of wholeness. Now moments of bright insight flash like fireflies lighting up a dark field on a warm summer night. Fireflies aren't lit all the time. Do they wonder, "Why aren't we lit all the time?" They are what they are, and they don't seem to find fault. They just light up in darkness; and whenever it happens the whole field sparkles luminously. What a wondrous way of being—for at least one moment not to find fault with anything! Not because it's a splendid idea, but because there is nothing to find fault with! There's only what is. And that's completely unbroken, without possibility of lack. Every one of us inevitably contributes to this unbroken, pulsating wholeness, whether we're temporarily good or bad, ignorant or wise, selfish or selfless, violent or gentle, beautiful or ugly personalities. All of us together, as we are, are an ever throbbing, ever changing, never gaining, never losing creative whole, floating in spaciousness that does not know right or wrong.

As personalities we have our idiosyncratic characteristics, habits, patterns, ways of responding. "Idiosyncrasy" literally means one's own peculiar blend. Different aspects of the whole are peculiarly blended in each one of us. Does this sound abstract, or can we begin to discern one total consciousness revealing itself through innumerable different expressions? We all have varying beliefs, changing views, different feelings, special experiences, personal ways of phrasing it—each one of us manifesting a particular mixture out of this totality of consciousness with its infinite possibilities.

19

Sexual Energy

*I*N A LETTER, someone wrote that "sexual energy can feel so powerful and so right at times, yet be so inappropriate in some situations." The person went on to say, "Not encouraging this energy seems to be most compatible with quiet simplicity and the preservation of order, stability, and primary relationship, but when it *does* appear, it can be so powerful and overwhelming—and feel right, whole, and needing to be honored." The person then asked whether one could deal honestly and openly with sexual energy. That is an interesting question.

Why can't we deal honestly and openly with sexual energy? When we feel aroused, is the sexual energy so overpowering physically and mentally that awareness is shut out?

Can there be times of quiet reflecting to question one's ingrained personal and collective ideas about sexuality—the ideas and images one has about oneself as a sexual being? Do I think of myself as sexually potent or not, in great need of sex or not, sexually attractive or not? Do I see the way in which I am affected in my desires by the social, religious, and media-culture stereotypes about sexuality? All the various attitudes, values, prohibitions, and social pressures around sex—does all of this conspire to prevent my looking at sexuality freely?

For instance, if an idea has been implanted in this body-mind that sexuality is undesirable and needs to be controlled or repressed, then sexuality cannot be openly examined. Neither can there be open questioning if I insist on an idea that having sex is absolutely necessary for my physical and mental well-being.

Can there be awareness of my many convictions and contradictory attitudes about sex as they emerge in different situations, with different people, at different times and places? It's not easy because convictions and contradictory feelings are part of our deep conditioning.

If by "dealing with sexuality" we mean *awaring* the fantasies, desires, sensations, emotions, and confusions we call "sexual energy"—not judging or identifying with what is observed but rather seeing it all openly—then everything can be honestly dealt with. *The seeing is the dealing.* Awareness has intrinsic wisdom that discerns what is and sees what leads to what. By that I mean intelligently observing and experiencing not only the sexual images, urges, physical arousal, and action taking place, but also some sustained awareness of the consequences of our actions—an intelligent recognition of the possessiveness that usually arises with romantic involvement with another person, the jealousies, anger, and hurt, as well as the addiction to repeating pleasures, at times at all cost.

Maybe now our fundamental question is: Can there really be sustained awareness in the presence of powerful sexual urges?

This is calling not for an answer but for attention. Thinking about it may only bring more confusion. But when interest in the question is powerful, then the energy to attend awakens by itself. And the first discovery may be that we do not really want to give attention at the time of sexual arousal. One doesn't really want to "deal" with it at all! The overwhelming impulse may be either to repress and control, or to abandon oneself, drowning in the delicious rapture of sensuality of an actual or fantasized encounter. (Even the "real" partner may be suffused with one's projected romantic imagery.) Attention at such moments may be felt to be a totally unwanted intrusion and instinctively denied.

But if a spark of awareness prevails, it may reveal how much conditioned imagery, how much memory and mental anticipation are involved in what is believed to be either genuine love or a purely biological, instinctive drive—our "chemistry."

One may find that without an internal video playing about the desired person and the consummation of romantic passion together, the biological drive does not maintain itself for long. No fuel, no fire! Cherished memories and anticipation of sound, smell, taste, touch, and sight keep the biology and chemistry of sex going. Clinging to the pleasurable memory of immersion in stimulation, and thus the craving for more, is probably the strongest fuel for the sexual fire.

Awareness does not carry anything with it—no thoughts, no judgment, no need, no control, no resistance. Awareness is not involved with results. It is not fuel. It simply sheds light that is wisdom and love. The question of how to "deal" with sexuality is moot. What more need be done than let awareness illuminate?

Life seems to be the expression of an inexhaustible desire to live and continue living in ever new and changing forms. The constantly renewing creativeness of life force, surging forth boundlessly in creatures playing, mating, pleasuring, fighting, killing, giving birth, caring for offspring while simultaneously serving as food for others, boggles the mind.

Sexual activity is a normal, infinitely creative function of all living forms, physically pleasurable to the senses and occurring in orderly rhythms and cycles. But for us humans, a large and complex brain makes it possible to store and generate alluring sexual fantasies capable of arousing the organism at any time, day or night, 365 days of the year, and into nonreproductive old age.

Most human beings feel lonely, separate, and alienated from each other, and the only possibility for at least a momentary joy of togetherness appears to lie in sexual union with its delights and self-abandonment. And yet there can also be that amazing awakening to our intrinsic wholeness beyond the sensuality of imagination and fantasy, revealing a vast stillness at the very core of this bustling existence. At a moment of touching this all-pervading, vibrant emptiness, our illusory isolation has disappeared. The ending of separation is love beyond imagination and sensual pleasure.

20

World Peace

OCCASIONALLY WE RECEIVE requests asking if we would be willing to join with other spiritual centers in dedicating a prayer, a chanting, or a retreat to world peace. Such a combined effort of focused energy, these requests suggest, would be a powerful experience and perhaps aid in promoting world peace and harmony.

Before immediately responding with a yes or no to such an appeal, could we inquire together into what we really mean when we speak about "the world" and "world peace"? Can we have some understanding about what is verbal, conceptual, and what is not? What is *the world*, and what is *peace?* Right now, as we are sitting here, is there a world, is there peace, or are these ideas of the thinking mind? What am I, what are we in relationship to the world and to world peace? Am I, as I know myself, real, or is this *I* an ever changing cluster of ideas, images, and sensations? Thinking conceptually, there appears to be a separation between me and the world, but is this separation actually true?

Over the years there have been many prayer meetings and meditations dedicated to world peace. Who is it that is praying, and what is the world that I am praying for? Are they truly different, forever separate, as the language implies and we believe, or are they fundamentally one seamless whole?

What is separation? Is it fact or is it deluded thinking?

When I was a child I fervently prayed to God, who I believed would protect me against all evil. I prayed for the safety of my family, particularly my mother. Not to let the house burn down—that was always included in my nightly prayer. When World War II broke out I prayed to God to prevent a bomb from hitting the huge smokestack located several blocks away. I imagined that if that thing toppled over in our direction, the tumbling bricks would destroy our house.

Did I pray for peace? I probably did but don't really remember today whether the concept of *peace* was meaningful then, because a horrendous war and the terror of persecution were raging endlessly, everywhere. So many millions of human beings were dying, being exterminated.

I remember the day my belief in a protective, loving God crumbled. During and after air raids I would usually feel depressed and forlorn. On that particular day, however, there was great activity throughout the house to put out a small fire in the attic. Actually my sister and I had been in bed with severe diarrhea all day long and went down into the cellar only when we heard some bombs falling. One of them ignited things in the house next door, and flames began jumping over into our fifth-floor attic. Suddenly all of us had plenty of energy to form a line of residents carrying buckets of water up the stairs and tossing them on the fire. We felt neither sickness, weakness, nor gloom. Nor did we think about war or peace. We just did what needed to be done and felt good when the flames dwindled and finally turned into smoke and ashes. The depression arrived later on when thoughts flooded the mind—thoughts about our perilous situation as a half-Jewish family, the dangers we were living through, and what could have happened or might happen in the next air raid—a future that was insecure, threatening, and deadly.

Whom could I possibly trust after all that had happened and was still happening? These events were totally incompatible with my idea of a loving God. The old faith vanished. Only the burning question remained: "What is the meaning of all this senseless chaos and intolerable suffering of human beings killing and killed by human beings? Does it have any meaning to be born into this vale of sorrow?" The question had an intense energy, kindling an urgency to find an answer that would give understanding and peace to this life filled with fear and darkness.

With the disturbing question about life's meaning, entirely new vistas began to open up. Sometimes when you are fording a stream you use rocks sticking out of the water to move from one spot to the next, leaving behind what you have stepped on. So it was like steps through the stream that things presented themselves to the searching mind: studies at a university, lots of books, talks with people, zazen at a Zen center, and exposure to the teachings of Krishnamurti. All these became catalysts for insights and further questioning without settling for any answer that was not beyond any shadow of doubt.

So—what is inner peace? I don't think that we can contribute anything to world peace unless we thoroughly understand the root of our own inner warring and confusion, which may be the origin of war and suffering in the world. Let's go easy on grasping for ideal states for the world, praying for peace on earth, without really clarifying the source of war and peace within this human being that I call myself. Can the delusion about me as a permanent and separate entity lift for just one instant? In moment-to-moment awareness one realizes the fleetingness of all the thoughts, memories, moods, and physical emotions I identify as myself. One sees the alternation of war and peace within oneself. One begins to learn about this brain-mind, totally interconnected with the entire organism and what we call the world. One sees how one thought alone can mobilize the entire body into mental and physical waves of fear, hostility, or hatred, demanding reprisal, defense, or attack. The next moment one may witness an entirely different thought kindling the desire to help people, to assist and to cherish them. We're talking about the way thoughts mobilize the energy to hate and to love.

Is there another energy that is not born of idea and thought (leaving aside the powerful drive to survive)?

An amazing energy is set free in seeing clearly what is taking place here right now, not through beliefs or ideas, but born of simple, immediate presence. Out of this wondrous presence flows right action that is not controlled by thoughts no matter how kind or unkind, how peaceful or contentious they may be. Seeing a fire can mobilize instant energy to put it out. Seeing a drowning person can move one to jump to the rescue. Immediate seeing is the energy of right action, with its wisdom and compassion.

So are we living separately from the world, or is the world simply a reflection of all our conditioned ways of living together throughout the millennia? Who am I to pray for this world that is a reflection of myself: at war with itself but also momentarily at peace, as when two people are seeing each other without any images and therefore without barriers, meeting together in simple goodness? The best moments of our lives happen when we respond without premeditation, out of the openness of our hearts, creating a space of peace and love.

Will we dedicate a retreat—a limited amount of time—to the ideal of world peace? Or can we live this moment of nowness by being fully here, in touch with the whole world as it is unfolding seamlessly from moment to moment?

Is that the first step—getting a glimpse of the inseparable wholeness of what I have called the world *and* me? Not merely an intellectual grasp, although that is better than thinking we are all isolated and divided from each other, either fighting each other endlessly or endeavoring to bridge a gap that doesn't really exist.

The tremendous realization that there *is* no separation dawns at the moment that the whole emotional network of stories about myself is quietly in abeyance, as though a plug was pulled. Being here with a clear, undisturbed mind is seeing the whole world as myself. Not as *me* or *mine* but as nothing divided—one community of an infinite variety of ever changing living beings.

When the mind is still in quiet presence, heaven and earth are open. Nothing is obstructing the view. A crow is calling—*caw caw caw caw*. Wind is stirring among the quivering leaves. Breath is flowing. No thought of world peace. Nothing to pray for. Everything is here just as it is, in an indescribable way.

Can we share this together right now, beyond words, beyond time?

PART FOUR

Conditioning and Wholeness

21

Is There Your Truth and My Truth, or Just One Truth?

WHAT IS TRUTH? Is there one unassailable truth, or are there many individual truths? Billions of truths? Because billions of human beings perceive things billions of different ways, according to their particular idiosyncrasies—blends.

As we talk together and each of us expresses different personal beliefs, points of view, and feelings, we cannot agree upon what's true. Heredity and past experiences vary for each of us, affecting present perceptions. We can't get together. We can't agree on what is true.

Can I get away from insisting on the truth of my individual perceptions and freely wonder whether truth exists irrespective of my own personal idiosyncrasies? Not truth according to *my* experiences, which are never the same as yours. *My* way of thinking and expressing needs to be open to questioning. What appears to be true today may not hold true tomorrow. Tomorrow we'll discover new galaxies never dreamt of before. So, as we talk together, can everything we say be open to questioning without self-protection? Do we get a glimpse now and then that all of us, just as we are, live in the same vast space?

We still haven't fully faced this fundamental question, What is truth? Just to repeat what the dictionary says, that it is "that which accords with reality," doesn't get us any place, because what is reality? Is reality all the things we see right now in this room? From your place over there you see different things than I do. If you are nearsighted you see differently from one who is farsighted. If you are blind you don't see with your eyes. And yet we're all sitting here together right now, quietly listening, being present. Aware.

Does it really matter what each one of us sees or doesn't see with the eyes? Objects don't really matter, do they?

What does matter—wonder of wonders—is the freedom of undivided being. If that's present—the openness of being without any identification, without any need to be somebody or become something—then does it matter what appears and disappears in awareness? A gurgling stomach, a bird calling, drifting clouds in the sky, breath flowing—it's all here! Everything is here. Nothing needs to be otherwise, nothing needs to be added or taken away, no need for anything to be better or worse. No need to relate to anything in any habitual way. No need to bring ourselves into the picture: "I see it well," or "I don't see it well enough." When thoughts like this occur, aren't they just another blip in this vast display? Nothing is interfering! There's just the utter simplicity of *being everything there is*, dispassionately aware. Is this truth?

The concept is not the real thing. And yet in a listening presence we can commune with each other freely, realizing that it's only attachment to our particular idiosyncrasies that seems to keep us apart. Can we see, together, that it is all conditioning? Come in touch with the peculiar mixtures in each other? Can we see that conditioning holds for all of us in our daily moment-to-moment interrelating?

Out of choiceless awareness, can we say clearly, "Yes, this is conditioned habit in me and in you." We can clearly feel the narrowing down when self-images arise. We can feel the fear, the hurt, a trembling confusion. What particular shape this is taking in you or me doesn't really matter. It's all one conditioning, one organism, one earth, one galaxy, one universe, one unbroken seamless whole.

In freely looking and listening at this moment, I don't know exactly what objects you may see or what sounds you may not hear. I've never seen with your eyes or heard with your ears. Particular ears and eyes don't matter right now. There is just total presence, expressing itself lovingly in empty space.

22

The Two Aspects of Meditative Inquiry

WHAT A BEAUTIFUL, quiet morning it is! The faint hum of insects, a cool breeze touching the skin.

The breathing—do we feel it? The body pulsating with heart beats. People sitting quietly together—are we here?

Is it essentially one whole listening, or are we locked into our private worlds of thinking, remembering, anticipating? Is there, for moments at a time, an open listening that does not create divisions among us? Can this humming, breathing, pulsating presence take the place of fantasizing, worrying, and wanting?

We are not asking in order to get rid of wanting or fearing; these cannot be gotten rid of by any conventional means. Our usual attempts to bring about change are analysis, judgment, condemnation, will power, control, and so on. But there is another, utterly simple way of being here. Just talking or reading about it isn't the same as entering deeply into it.

Published under the title "Utterly Simple: A Sunday Talk with Toni Packer" in *Shambhala Sun,* March 2001. Reprinted with permission.

Right now can there be simple listening, awaring, being present to what appears as sound and feeling and thinking in the midst of open silence? A vast listening space of no preferences and no judgments—no one here to *do* the listening. It's happening on its own.

So why do we sit down, alone and together, in motionless stillness? Why do we sit down, go on retreat, time and time again?

We usually sit down with all kinds of intentions and expectations that seldom correspond to what is actually taking place from moment to moment. For a few people a sense of stillness comes readily; but often in the course of sitting there arise thoughts and feelings of boredom, dullness, disappointment, and frustration. Then comes the inevitable question, Why am I doing this? What is it good for anyway? The intellect wants to grasp the purpose of meditative work.

Different answers are given by different traditions, and the practices used to still the mind vary. But why have a special practice? Of course, one may wish to continue with a previously learned practice. Or maybe be open to trying something new: simply attending without a known method or purpose. Attending to what is taking place from moment to moment isn't a technique—it is what is and that is all!

Simplicity is the essence of this work. How do we keep it simple? Can we detect and leave aside the complications created by thinking how things *ought* to be?

There are two aspects of quiet sitting, or meditative inquiry, if you will, which are not mutually exclusive. Description and language divide what is indivisible. So maybe we can keep in mind that what is being described separately right now is one complete whole.

One aspect of meditation is becoming intelligently aware of what we call our conditioning, our habitually unconscious or semi-conscious reactions toward each other and the situations around us. We may think we are aware (in the sense that all human beings are "conscious"), but we are not really in touch with true, undivided awareness. True awareness has no element of judging, analyzing, rejecting, or clinging. No *me*-center from which to observe, but awareness shedding light, bringing the *me* into fresh view.

Meditation is coming into intimate touch with our habitual reactions of fear, desire, anger, tenderness, or whatever, discovering them freshly, abstaining from automatically judging them good or bad, right or wrong. Beginning to realize that every incident, every encounter with another person, is instantly interpreted according to ingrained prejudices. There is constant comparing ourselves and others to ideal standards of good and bad and right and wrong, that have been internalized long ago.

At a moment of insight there arises a new sense of wondering: "Why do we live bogged down in automatic reactions? Is it the only way of relating in this world?" Will we be seduced into explaining or philosophizing about it, or can we simply stay with what is going on in the light of the question? Genuine interest has a way of kindling energy to illuminate automatic reactions—for instance, immediately getting hurt because of a critical remark, and instantly defending or paying back, and then mulling the whole affair over and over—which are alienating and cause suffering for us all.

Obviously, not everything that is possible to think about, feel, or experience will come up in one sitting, one day, or even one retreat! Let's just look and listen to what *does* appear and never mind what doesn't. Watch the images with their connected emotions that grip us tightly, images about how good we are or how bad, and how good or bad others are.

(I'm putting it in simple terms—images about ourselves and others are numberless and each one of us can fill in what we see.) All kinds of ideas and assumptions float around in the mind. Not that they *shouldn't* be there, but rather do we detect them and see them in a new light of understanding? Is there a dawning realization that fantasies take over the bodymind, creating desire and fear time and time again? Can it be caught directly, discovering the instant link between fantasy and desire? Maybe there is a feeling of dullness in sitting, and fantasy kicks in about being somewhere else that's more entertaining. I may imagine myself in a beautiful place with an exhilarating friend, and relish the internal show unfolding away from this present place of lackluster tedium. Then, momentarily coming out of the fantasy, can we leave judgment aside and instantly touch what is actually going on right now? What is it that I have labeled as "dullness"? Can I listen to it gently, sounding it out intimately? With closer attention I may sense an uncomfortable lack of excitement like a withdrawal craving for stimulation, and underneath it a vague sense of restlessness and fear. Can we ask ourselves what it is all about—not with the intellect, but by letting the inner feelings with their story lines reveal themselves as they are?

Sooner or later, we may discern the palpable difference between just being here as we are, openly attentive, and the state of entanglement in a web of fantasy about being somewhere else. Can we directly experience this difference without a need to elevate or disparage either state? Every state of being speaks for itself.

In awareness the stimulation of muscles, organs, or glands proceeds normally, keeping the body alive and wholesome. With fantasy, a shift occurs. Fantasy, with its story lines, mobilizes the body into chains of reaction. We have firmly believed that *we* (separate entities) are in control of ourselves and are the initiators of actions, choosing what to do and what not to do. But now, to our surprise or frustration, we discover that there is no one who has *chosen* to react. Reaction is as instantaneous as a conditioned reflex. There is no intervening entity—just thoughts and physical responses connecting together automatically.

A little while ago a Buddhist journal devoted some space to prisoners on death row. One of the prisoners, convicted for multiple rapes and murder, wrote an article expressing his deep gratitude for having been given a medication that radically reduces testosterone. The drug relieved him of horrendous fantasies that used to drive him to action mercilessly. Relieved of the fantasies, he felt no compulsion to act out. The instant we understand people the way they are, our actions are no longer compelled by obsessive thoughts and stereotypes entangling this burdened mind and body.

Recently, on public television, there was a segment about present movie trends stereotyping Muslims as terrorists. A number of recent movies feature attacks upon American cities in which the terrorists are all Muslims/Arabs. One scene shows Muslims praying in the mosque, and in the next scene whole blocks of buildings are exploding into fire and smoke. An interviewer asked the man who reviewed the movies if he could recall any movie in recent years in which Arabs and Muslims are presented in a positive light. He said he could not. He did mention that over the years there has been much improvement in not stereotyping other ethnic groups such as Indians, African-Americans, Chinese, and Jews, but presently Arabs and Muslims are the target.

Is there an inner resistance to looking at the way we really are? We don't have a problem with being friendly and helpful. But coming into direct touch with the way we often think, talk, and react—self-centered, prejudiced, intolerant, and frequently violent—can be very painful. Will we cling to comforting self-images of being good and right—or will we see ourselves clearly, without deception? This could be like a ray of sunlight shining through the clouds.

The other aspect of quiet meditation is the wonder of coming upon that which is not conditioned, that which is beyond fantasy and remembrance. Sitting quietly, without desire and fear, beyond the sense of time, is vast, boundless being, not belonging to you or me. It is free and unattached, shedding light on conditioned being, beholding it and yet not meddling with it. The seeing is the doing. *Seeing* is change. It is not what is seen that matters, but that there is seeing, revealing what is as it is, in the light of wisdom and compassion too marvelous to comprehend.

23

Consciousness, Attention, and Awareness

*T*HIS MORNING BIRDS ARE CHIRPING and a distant saw is buzzing. Is the listening simple, open, or is the mind occupied with other things?

The sound of sawing reminds me of California, where the retreat house is surrounded by tall eucalyptus trees lining the streets and adjacent lots. One year a strong windstorm had felled many trees and torn off limbs that were strewn about. Workers were busy cutting up the wood, and their chain saws were screeching stridently. A few people got upset because their silent retreat was being disturbed. One energetic woman called the president of the neighboring college, where a lot of sawing was going on that day, asking whether the saws could be stopped for a while as we were in a retreat and had paid a lot of money for silence. Graciously he obliged, and the saws fell silent for a while. What a relief it was—no more grinding on the nerves. Most of the time, however, we live under conditions that grate on our nerves and we cannot make a phone call to stop it!

How do we live with disturbance when it cannot be changed? Is it possible to live without getting upset and angry so quickly? No need to answer yes or no, or think that I would be able to do that if I were more attentive. Not taking any position, can we simply listen, quietly watching inwardly what else is going on besides the grating sounds around us? (Sometimes people feel disturbed by someone breathing heavily next to them.) I don't mean listening to anything in particular, such as birdsong, airplanes, or saws—not listening to anything in specific detail. Just an unfolding openness that makes it possible to become aware of inner reactions, such as thinking, "My long-awaited retreat is being wrecked—I hate all this noise!" Watching attentively and learning how instantaneously incendiary thoughts arouse anger and keep it going, and how story and anger can also dissolve into quiet space.

Is it possible to purify perception by beholding clearly what distorts it? Mental, verbal, and physical reactions arouse emotions that dull our perceptions—this can be directly experienced by all of us. When we are upset we do not listen properly. But dullness can give way to clarity when resentment and resistance are directly exposed, felt, and seen to be a hindrance.

Actually, quite a number of retreatants mentioned that they learned a lot from having to listen to these grating chain saws. We learn to our surprise that annoyance can be replaced by presence—not getting sucked into an upsetting story. Maintaining awareness. Not resisting whatever disturbance presents itself.

Not resisting? Do we know what that means? Not resisting. Yielding. Directly, vulnerably experiencing what is here, together with all the gross and subtle ways that this body-mind has cultivated to brace itself against the pain and agony of disturbance, condemning it, battling it, or even shutting down to avoid feeling it altogether. It is the miracle of presence that makes our inner processes transparent and light with awareness. This is what happens—awareness revealing what is going on, taking the place of a habit that is vulnerably exposed. It is not that I drop the habit. Sometimes people say, "I ought to drop this habit, but I can't." No one is asking us to drop anything. How can we drop things when we are in our customary thinking and suffering mode? We can drop a bowl of cereal, but our habitual reactions need to be seen thoroughly as they are taking place. When there is awareness, a reaction that is seen and understood to be a hindrance diminishes on its own. It may take a lot of repeated suffering, but a moment comes when the energy of seeing takes the place of the habit. That is all. Seeing is empty of self. The root of habit too is empty.

Is there any difference between *consciousness, attention,* and *awareness?* Are those terms synonymous? I sometimes use *awareness* and *attention* synonymously, and some spiritual teachers use the word *consciousness* the way I use *awareness.*

First of all, do we see clearly that words are only words and can be used in different ways? It is important to understand how we are using words in talking together right now, agreeing on their intellectual meaning, and having some direct insight into what they are actually pointing at.

Can we use the word *consciousness* to encompass the whole movement of thinking, reflecting, imagining, remembering, projecting, anticipating, knowing, and all the feelings and emotions connected with that? When we say, "I'm feeling self-conscious right now," we mean that we are thinking about ourselves according to conditioned self-images and that we are feeling hemmed in. We may have been conditioned to think positively about ourselves, an action that generates good feelings, or negatively, churning with self-deprecation. Most of the time we do a mixture of both. Can it be verified directly that all thoughts about oneself affect the physical chemistry of this organism in one way or another?

Consciousness isn't just thinking about myself—it is thinking about you and about the world, all created by remembered impressions, thinking about them, imagining and combining experiences in narrative ways. A head full of ever changing stories about what I am like, what people are like, what they are thinking about me, and what the world is like. Sometimes we say: "What is this world coming to? How terrible it is!" or "How magnificently beautiful!" Our stories always change, sometimes from one moment to the next. When thoughts are pleasant, when things are going well and a nagging problem has been resolved, the world looks good. But let a new problem arise and grip this bodymind, and who even cares about the world! When we are soaked in problems we are too preoccupied to notice anything.

So not only is consciousness what we think about ourselves, but it also comprises our entire thought-created world—a different world picture for each one of us depending on our circumstances, accumulated history, and weather-like moods. As long as we are living ensconced in our private virtual reality, we feel isolated. We separate ourselves from each other through our thought-produced worlds.

By *consciousness*, then, we mean a thought-created reality with the *me*-thought in the center of it. *Me* as knowledge, as memory, as image, as history.

Then there is attention. For right now, we'll define it as having a focus—paying attention *to* birdsong, *to* chainsawing, *to* breathing, *to* eating, walking, sitting, talking, resting, thinking, emoting. To do anything well we have to pay attention to what we are doing—concentrating energy on this rather than that, learning not to get distracted. Learning to be attentive permeates most spiritual training: giving minute attention to one's moment-to-moment activities, be it listening, thinking, washing, dressing, eating, defecating, driving the car, speaking, walking, paining, or pleasuring. Noticing how things feel, how food tastes, how one's hands and body move in cleaning the floor, how thoughts trigger emotions and emotions generate thoughts.

Let me take a moment to look at a possible pitfall in attention training. Thinking back to my own practice time at a Zen center, I remember that we were all fairly good at being attentive. I don't want to speak for others, but I personally was very self-conscious about maintaining my concentration. I knew I was attentive in moving about and felt good about that accomplishment, even proud. I noticed when people were watching me and imagined that they were approving of my attentiveness. From our earliest days on we have learned to live in the eyes of others, seeking their approval, admiration, and love. Any new skill that we learn can serve as a fresh opportunity to win approval and avoid blame.

Even though I learned to be attentive in certain required ways, I was paying far less attention to what else was going on in this bodymind. There wasn't an intelligent awareness of thoughts about myself—that there was always *someone* being attentive *to* something.

Once before a round of sitting a man was standing in front of my seat putting on his cardigan, meticulously guiding each button through its hole. He proceeded very slowly with great attention, right in front of my eyes, while not noticing that several people were piling up behind him waiting to get to their seats. The brain is constantly creating images in terms of what we are doing and whether it is approved or not. I couldn't ask the man about this at that time, but maybe he was picturing himself as an attentive meditator. Attachment to self-images prevents simple awareness. Like children who are used to getting attention by demonstrating their accomplishments, we may find ourselves thinking:

"Watch me! Do you see how attentive I am? Do you approve of me?" Like anything else, being attentive can become a self-centered activity that is cultivated because we think it is meritorious in the eyes of others.

What is awareness?

It cannot possibly be defined. It is easier to point out what is *absent* in awareness. It is not self-conscious—it does not think about itself. It does not think! Only consciousness thinks. Awareness is not a product of thought or imagination. It does not have a self-center. In an unfathomable way, it sheds light on consciousness, on self-centered activity. Not judgmentally, not condemning or accepting what reveals itself. Just illuminating, making transparent what is unfolding this moment. Awareness has no inner division, no outer boundaries. No *inner* and no *outer*. It is true being, beholding everything out of the emptiness of no self. *Emptiness* is not a concept here. It reveals itself effortlessly when willing, wanting, resisting, grasping are in abeyance. Awareness reveals all these movements as conditioned reactions.

The question comes up frequently: Is there such a thing as partial awareness? At times I use the term "partial awareness" to point to a nonjudgmental witnessing or experiencing of a strong habit that keeps running in spite of seemingly coming into awareness. Is this really open awareness, as we are using that word, or is it suffused with wanting, judging, feeling, and processing? Sometimes I think that a quick alternation may be taking place between awareness and the compulsive running of habitual thought and emotion. It feels like partial awareness—I'm aware of what's going on, but the habit doesn't stop. It's as if something inside doesn't want to stop, look, and listen completely.

Let's take an innocuous example of observing a craving: I feel a strong desire for eating chocolate. It's an old habit to eat chocolate after a meal. The mind is actively visualizing the candy that has given great pleasure in the past, and the mouth is salivating at the thought of it. The desire increases with each image of actually putting a piece of chocolate into the mouth, chewing it, and tasting its delicious flavor. There is also some fleeting awareness in all of this. It can intensify if I'm really curious about what is going on. With sufficient interest and the energy that it generates, awareness can actually replace the compulsion of desire with simple presence. At such a moment there is an unexpected freedom. Compulsion to eat or not to eat chocolate is absent—the bodymind is open. Most of the time, however, we do not want to interrupt a pleasurable sequence with anything, and the desired thing is pursued and consumed with great gusto.

Let me say here that short of making ourselves sick, a lot of our habits like eating chocolate are harmless, in that they do not cause suffering for ourselves or others by running their course. But the question is not really what habits are harmful and which ones are not, but whether our moment-to-moment living can take place with awareness of what is going on. Can there be a wakeful stopping and listening as we are getting hurt or angry over someone's critical comment, as we are hurting others with our own cynical remark, as fear arises and mobilizes the bodymind, as we are sucked into story lines that trigger anger and resentment? Can we wake up to our deeply conditioned inner restlessness that grips us when we are idle—awaring the lurking feeling that we ought to do something in order not to feel guilty and useless?

Do we feel curiosity about the ways of our habits, feel some urgency to watch them impartially, without the compulsion to move along with them? This stopping and wondering is the amazing power of presence. It has nothing to do with renunciation, with ideas of right and wrong. It's simply stopping and wondering dispassionately what strong physical or emotional reactions are all about. It's not about whether or not to eat chocolate, to smoke a cigarette, or make a cynical joke—it is finding out firsthand about the blind drivenness of our reactions in the wondrous power of presence. A shift can take place from our thought-propelled motion to simply being here, waking up from the dream of the moment, and at the same time beginning to realize how persuasively the brain provides fuel for the fulfillment of our desires by spinning out scenarios, excuses, rationalizations, encouragement. There is no need to judge any of this as right or wrong. There is no right or wrong, only what is happening as it's happening—simply beholding the movements of this amazing bodymind in motionless presence.

24

Is Presence Available Everywhere?

S OMEONE SAID, "In listening to your talk, not so much to the words but experiencing the energy that is manifesting, I realized that stillness is not just the quietness of the mind. It's not just the absence of thoughts. Stillness is an immense energy without any boundaries. Why don't you talk about that?" Someone else commented, "You talk so much about all the thoughts and stuff we get caught up in, but you don't talk about this amazing stillness—the freedom from all the stuff. Why not?"

My first response was, "It's early in the retreat, only the second day." Well, maybe something that is so close, that is the source of oneself, the ground of everything, including speaking, is hard to talk about. Let it speak for itself, this tremendous energy of presence, being here completely open and in touch! It is nothing that you can see. Seeing itself is presence without borders.

A number of people asked, "Does this energy of stillness manifest everywhere? Is it accessible at any place the way it is accessible here right now?"

This is the question for all of us, isn't it? Can it be accessed anywhere, or is it only in special places that humankind has cultivated over the millennia, special spots where we contact energy beyond the struggle of our daily life with its trials and tribulations?

This may not be just a theoretical question. We yearn to access the energy of stillness wherever we are because we realize that in being present there is no division. There is peace and harmony. I don't mean the greeting card variety of peace and harmony—sometimes it's understood only in this sentimental way.

Is this question alive in daily life as we get involved in conflict and argument, in self-absorption, in comparing ourselves with others? Is this question alive this moment? Where is this energy now, the stillness? Is it here?

Or is there an overwhelming drive to go on with having to win, having to be right, needing to know, to become, to be better than others? All these powerful currents of habit! Like the smog that hides what is there all the time.

We live in smog so much of our daily lives, not just suffering from it but amazingly attached to it. As somebody said in a dialogue, "I don't want to let go of delusion. It's my existence!" It's not a rational decision to hold on to a habit— the involuntary grip of attachment to our bondage can be directly experienced.

We spend so much time in retreat taking a closer look at the smog because the smog is what we live in most of the time. Can we wonder, "What are its ingredients?" Not settle for wishing to regain the clarity we experienced in retreat last time. Such desires only add to the smog. That's thinking and wanting and fearing without attending right now to what's here right in front of our eyes.

Can this question about the availability of quiet presence catch fire right in the midst of mental and physical smog? In the midst of what we are holding on to, what we're afraid of giving up? Clearly feel the power of these currents of habit! See the urge to go on with the pleasure or pain. See the competitive striving, the constant comparing ourselves with others. See it freshly, in a new light. Is that possible? Right in the midst of it. Often it happens afterward, but we're asking, Is it possible to see it while we're right in it? And stop for a moment? Wake up, look, and listen!

Unless we are genuinely interested in waking up to what is happening, habit continues. What tremendous drive and power and energy are in these smoggy habits!

At the moment of involvement, in the habitual need to be right, to fight the wrong or to protect oneself—can there be an instant of silence, a fresh energy, a peaceful presence? Is it here now? To stop for a moment, just enough to see whether it's possible to stop?

Habitual thinking says, I have a choice. I could either stop or go on. But do I really have a choice? We're trying to find out what this *I* is that creates all the confusion. So we ask whether at this moment of feeling the current of habit—the pleasure or pain of it—we can stop and not need to go on, in spite of the tremendous push and pull of that current. There is something that is not of this pushing and pulling current, something that just sheds light.

People tell me about habits that are difficult to control or to give up, and yet something in each person must be aware of the habits to be able to describe them. A person this morning mentioned that no matter how still it is, how present, there is still the observer. And with that observer comes the distance, the division: "me here" observing "that over there." The question that came up was, "What is aware of the observer?" There was not much thought activity, the person reported, just awaring the division between observer and whatever was experienced. Does thought habitually think that there *must* be an observer because something is seen? Can there be awareness without an observer?

Awareness is here—so immediate, so present, and yet so amazingly ignored. Not taken seriously because we are deeply involved in what we are seeing, what we are desiring, and what it is we are afraid of. Awareness is here in spite of our ignorance. Future and past are just thought. The thinking, sensing, emoting, tensing is the smog. This amazingly agile organism responds to the slightest stirring of a thought. One thought occurs, and instantly wanting and fearing manifest throughout the body. It doesn't take more than one thought. But it is rarely just one thought. One thought gives birth to another and another and another. And thus desire and fear are maintained and carried, and nerve connections are constantly strengthened for the whole process to repeat itself again and again.

In the midst of all of this, awareness is here, isn't it? The immense, serene energy of stillness, too marvelous to describe—it is all there is. It is here whether we realize it or not.

25

Stillness and Openness

SOMEONE ASKED, "Is there a difference between stillness, when the mind quiets down and becomes silent at times but the *me* continues, and openness (open awareness), in which the sense of *me* is absent? In stillness the sense of *me* is still operating."

Words can be used arbitrarily—all we need is agreement on their meaning. Right now the questioner defines *stillness* as a state of being in which a subtle sense of *me* is felt. For the moment we'll go along with that definition.

What is the difference between open awareness without any sense of *me*, and stillness in which the *me* is subtly at work? It is a good question—a lot of people ask it. And then some people don't want to ask it because there is an attachment to stillness, in which thought uses subtle control to keep itself intact and going. The bodymind has learned how to "produce" stillness. Are control mechanisms at work? Find out by wondering and watching. One may not want to be disturbed in one's precious stillness, resisting the question whether or not the *me* is clinging to this stillness.

What could be the motive for making an effort to produce stillness and trying to hold on to it? Is this question itself disturbing stillness? Can we look and listen inwardly? Who or what is getting disturbed? Can one question this, even if the questioning seems to break up the stillness? In the true stillness that we are calling *open awareness*, questions can be asked and explored quietly without creating a disturbance.

So let us ask ourselves if there is a motive to use stillness in order to avoid something disturbing or painful. Are we pushing for or bracing against something in order to remain in stillness, or is the body at ease and open, ready to meet whatever may be happening from moment to moment?

Sometimes, to one's amazement, the *me*-center is just not there. Actually, it is not a natural ingredient of true being. The sense of *me* overlays the clear water of pure being like colorful layers of oil constructed by thought and memory. And there is nothing right or wrong with it, nothing that needs to be excused, fought, or conquered. Those kinds of efforts are the *I* working for and against itself and thereby subtly renewing and strengthening itself. We don't have to get rid of anything—just remain dispassionately and compassionately aware of whatever is taking place. Whatever arises—fear, anger, joy, boredom—let it be. It changes like the weather. One doesn't really know what anything is if thought does not label it this or that, good or bad, right or wrong. What is this fleeting moment without any story line spinning it out in time, without any evaluations or judgments? That is a fundamental question. Let it sit here without trying to answer it immediately. At times the truth about oneself simply reveals itself, one knows not why or how. One hasn't done a thing to bring it about!

Open awareness right now means no *me*-center grasping or objecting. Moods, feelings, sensations are simply what they are. Joy, sadness, elation, depression, crickets chirping, birds twittering, inhaling, exhaling—let it be. Let it all happen right here. No inside and no outside, no good and no bad. These are all concepts, aren't they? Listen freshly—breathing, chirping, touching, seeing—one unfathomable whole. Awaring it all—no one doing it. The emptiness of no center.

Don't make a concept or a picture out of what is being said—a picture is *not* what is.

There is a little book by Vimala Thakar entitled *Beyond Awareness*. Of course, the mind plays with anything and speculates: "What could be beyond awareness?" "Beyond awareness" simply means dropping it all; having no idea; nothing; just what is here from moment to moment. Not giving any special importance to it.

Just what is here as it is. Beholding it all in empty wonderment.

26

Is Awareness Enough?

WAKING UP DURING THE NIGHT and looking out the window, such bright stars! The earth is enveloped in a fresh, white blanket of innocence. No footprints yet. No car tracks. No dirt. An amazing thing—everything wiped clean. Like turning over a new leaf.

Yesterday I said, "Awareness is not enough." Why did I say that, some people were asking. Feeling the pain and sadness with tears welling up at memories of my late husband, Kyle, I said, "Awareness is not enough." As I said it I wondered if someone would ask me about that. Somebody did. I do need to say more about what I meant at the time. Feeling loss and pain and grief and sadness, one realizes how instantaneously remembrance creates a surge of sensations and emotions. Memories and physical reverberations are as one—it seems as though nothing could interrupt that immediate connection. Awareness appears to be there, but the remembering-paining-grieving cycle does not cease just because of it. And that's all right. Awareness is like a mirror that shows what is happening, what we are at this instant, the joy and grief, pain and well-being, turmoil and peacefulness. Awareness reveals these memory connections but no one intending or creating them. There is no *I* to be found directing things—there is only what has been described.

What does it mean, "Awareness is not enough?"

Where is our true abiding place at the rock bottom of everything—an immovable presence? Is it just in the fleeting flow of events, both external and internal—the thoughts, the feelings and emotions, the organism's reverberations—and moving along with it all? Or is it simply *awaring* it all?

A crucial shift takes place when the "anchoring" is not in the flowing with what is taking place, not getting identified with it as *me* and *mine* but remaining with simple awareness. Letting what is happening come and go on its own, without moving with it. Do we see the difference between moving with ephemeral events like sensations and upsets, and an immovable presence? It's for each of us to come upon that utter stillness, that unshakable stability of awareness in which change happens, in which thoughts, pains, and joys are allowed to come and go freely, without interference. No urge to judge good and bad, no need to feel guilty, no compulsion to rationalize anything away. Presence is awareness that is unflappable, no matter what it reveals about us. And in finding this spot—it's not really a spot, it's timeless space—there is peace. Absence of conflict. Absence of resistance, of struggle and striving. The amazing grace of no wanting and fearing. Love.

Someone said, "I was puzzled when you said it's inevitable that a memory triggers physical reaction. Why did you say it's inevitable?" Remembering Kyle, the loss of him, the yearning to have him back, and the realization that he is gone forever causes instantaneous surges of pain throughout the body. When it's happening it seems inevitable. It comes with such incredible speed! It *is* inevitable as long as there isn't this deep, motionless awareness-presence. In its seeming absence the *me*-network operates inexorably with all its past history, its agony, longing, and paining. But when awareness is effortlessly present without a trace of obstruction or doubt, a memory about Kyle's death and dying does not trigger any painful physical reverberations. It is an amazing discovery! Awareness can short-circuit the deeply established, conditioned connections of the bodymind. The spark of memory does not inevitably ignite grief and pain, anger or hurt. It remains the light of awareness.

It does not happen like that when there is just *witnessing awareness*, a seemingly separate "witness" observing what is going on in our moment-to-moment living. Witnessing awareness has an important place. It's significant to witness how automatically we react, how we dream and yearn for the past to appear again in the future. How we want things to be different from the way they are and the suffering this entails. It's crucial to learn about it all, so there is a foundation of thoroughly understanding our conditioned, reflexive mind and its self-deceptions.

We try to seek for that clarity, we endeavor to find an anchor underneath everything. But that is only chasing after ideas. Clear seeing does not see itself—it just illuminates the constant motion of conditioning without moving itself. It hides as long as we are willfully searching for it. Let it manifest on its own! Let it reveal the ten thousand facets of our conditioned self—the manner in which we react defensively, the way we talk to each other both politely or angrily, generously or enviously, the fears we are afraid to touch, the jealousy we don't want to face, the kindness and compassion that surfaces without any intention. This is meditation no matter where we are—being in touch with the thoroughly conditioned human mind. It's the same in all of us even though the contents of our individual experiences and their interpretations vary infinitely.

We all live in memory, in imagery, in ideas and fantasy about ourselves and each other, in constant wanting and fearing that distort the truth of what is actually going on right now. This phenomenon seems to be universal. It is the function of the brain to create picture maps of our world, so it can assume that it has reliable knowledge about what's dangerous and what is safe, what brings pleasure and what causes pain. At times it may be fairly accurate; at other times, it's totally off the mark. What is known and fantasized about other human beings and ourselves has little base in reality. It may all be dream work. But it all turns out to be surprisingly open to wondering and questioning. It can even be short-circuited by a presence that defies all description.

What is this presence, this awareness we talk about so much? Someone in a group discussion said, "I've noticed that most of the time when I think I'm aware, I'm in fact only thinking about myself." How true! That's why I like to differentiate between consciousness and awareness.

Consciousness is everything that has to do with thinking about me and you and the world—remembering, anticipating, resisting, desiring, fearing—all according to what we know from past experience, the entire field of knowledge. And this consciousness, as it is operating, can reveal itself in awareness. As it is.

Consciousness is the act of spinning the web of thinking, the web of *me* and *you* and *the world*, with all its feelings and emotions. It is a web spun from thought.

Question it, test it out. Don't believe it just because Toni is saying it. Don't accept me as an authority. That's more thinking. Can you test it out for yourself, directly?

If something is truly seen for an instant—how we just

reacted automatically and how thought is taking over, can that simply come into awareness? If you say, "Most of the time I'm thinking about myself," is that more thinking, or is it a direct discovery?

Awareness is like the sun shining through the clouds.

One aspect of meditating, retreating, or just living our daily lives is to come directly in touch with what is happening in ourselves and around us, going beyond the verbiage and imagery and seeing how we are entangled in it. Awareness has its own wise action—not different from love and compassion.

The other aspect is to come in touch with stillness that doesn't move, awareness that doesn't judge, that needs no objects. It needs nothing.

People ask, "Would I be aware if there was nothing to be aware of?" Yes! Awareness needs no object. No subject *I*! Objects come and go and may even stay away in the depth of meditation. It doesn't matter. What matters is presence, awareness, in which there is no fragmentation, no division, no *me* here and "everybody else" out there. All that is mind-made stuff. It needs to be seen as such.

Let me answer questions that may be lingering right now in people's minds: Does meditation mean I need to quiet down and be without thoughts? Does it mean I need to see everything about myself?

It's both. It's neither. It is without *I*.

In seeing the hills and valleys now shrouded in fog, now lit up by sunlight—do we see the *ideas* about them, or is there just unlimited space in which things freely appear and disappear? The open space being oneself, and what appears and disappears oneself, without division.

27

Enlightenment

OMEONE ASKED, "Does it really matter if we 'wake up' or not?"

A little while ago I took a walk up the hill. What a delightful morning! Warmth and coolness were present at the same time. Gentleness pervaded the air, and birds were singing everywhere. Wet, sodden shoes passed by the croaking pond where tiny little skimmers crisscrossed back and forth on the surface of the water, leaving their ever so delicate tracks.

On the big upper field several deer were grazing. Looking up at the intruder, their long white tails twitched a little as we looked at each other. Then they kept on grazing. Colors dotted the sun-drenched field, and blooming grasses were swaying in the breeze. The fragrance of wild roses filled the air.

If you had walked along with me this beautiful morning, we both would have laughed at the question whether it matters if we wake up or not.

Had we been caught up in anger, worry, or frustration, we wouldn't have laughed. We would not have seen the lovely vibrant field.

We have so many questions. Whence do they arise? Are there deeper motives to our question? Can we wonder about it and look? Someone asked, "Is there such a thing as ultimate, complete, and total enlightenment?" Are we really asking, "If there is such a thing, can I get it?"

Where does wondering about complete and total enlightenment come from? And from where does wanting it arise? And the frustration about not getting it? Doesn't it all come out of our deep inner discontent with ourselves, with others, and with the world? Sometimes we can't even say what it is that causes it; we just feel painfully out of sync. There is an inner meaninglessness, a feeling of hollow emptiness. Not the emptiness of vast open space, but a feeling of nothing of value inside, feeling lonely, cut off from happiness and alienated from people. There may be the fear of abandonment, or feeling unloved. All of these things are going on in human beings.

Out of the desire to fill up the inner depletion and find lasting contentment may come questions about enlightenment, and with them the yearning to find meaning and not feel isolated from everything and everyone. The brain creates endless concepts and fantasies to alleviate the inner suffering.

If we become increasingly transparent to these movements of thought and feeling, we will realize that inner pain is not dissolved by conventional ways of dealing with it, materially or spiritually. Money, position, acquisitions, or relationships have not brought lasting contentment. Religious beliefs may provide illusions of security and support, but for many of us they simply have not worked. We have wandered from one belief system to another, attracted by promises of salvation, liberation, or enlightenment, but real hunger for truth and clarity can be stilled only with genuine food.

The discursive mind is capable of throwing up doubts

and skeptical questions at any time. Maybe we suddenly find ourselves in quiet openness, a profound stillness without any feeling of lack. Then thought comes in and begins to wonder: "Will this last? Can I get it back? Was it real? Was this enlightenment or is there more? It doesn't seem enough." Thinking about a past moment of freedom immediately sows the seeds of doubt by asking, "Is this all there is? It can't be! There must be a more convincing experience than what I just had!" Thoughts grow like clinging vines that choke the living presence. Truly being here is being unknown, unknowable, unadorned. Being here is absence of doubting or affirming thoughts about myself. It is the absence of me! Thoughts that arise about me are just thoughts, with their enormous power to obscure clarity.

Is it our task to find out whether or not there is total and complete enlightenment like the Buddha proclaimed? I always liked the Buddha's saying: "I truly attained nothing from complete, unexcelled enlightenment, and that is why it is called complete, unexcelled enlightenment." *No-thing,* no one to attain it, spaceless space, no one there to occupy it. Just alive presence with the evening star in the sky. Dying to all the stuff imagined and clung to about oneself—what I am, what I was, what I will be, what I could be, should be . . .

Can we see all concepts *as concepts* with deepening clarity and wisdom? Not immediately lurching toward something promised in the future that has its sole existence in thought? Can we clearly discern what constitutes thinking and what is actually present right here without needing to think it? Can we discern it effortlessly?

The open windows, fresh air touching the skin, bright sunshine everywhere, all kinds of twittering sounds, crows calling and breathing, pulsating life! *Caw, caw, caw, caw . . .* Sensations throughout the body, breathing, beholding it, not the words, but the aliveness of it all. Can we realize now that "complete unexcelled enlightenment" is a concept?

You may sincerely object, "How can I know for sure that enlightenment is just a concept? Maybe it *is* real. Lots of enlightened teachers have told and written about it. So— shall we then ask together: "What is enlightenment beyond all concepts?"

Let us delve profoundly into this question, not asking for other people's descriptions of experiences, not looking for promises, not expecting to know for sure, but questioning out of not knowing, inquiring meditatively, deeply, darkly, until we don't know anymore what is "enlightened" or "unenlightened"! In silently wondering deeply without knowing, the conceptual world is left behind. Are we going into the question in this way?

All too often our yearning for something to alleviate the inner suffering gets in the way of deep inquiry. Rather than asking, "What is enlightenment?" can we question our inner feeling of insufficiency? We have tried to fill it with fantasies of all descriptions, with entertainment, acquisitions, achievements, relationships, spiritual searching, and solemn vows— anything to fill the aching void. But have we ever really explored it directly, unconditionally?

Becoming conscious of it in or out of retreat, can we be with the ache of emptiness, not calling it by any name? Let all labels fly into thin air and stay with what is here, discomfort without calling it discomfort. Staying here with what's indefinable. Not resisting, not fighting, not looking for anything else. Just letting what is here be here in its entirety, physically, mentally, totally. Letting it be without knowing. Not becoming the doer for or against it. Just this quiet presence in the midst of the silence of chaos. In this there is an unfolding transparency. It happens when one sits patiently, silently, unconditionally. By "sitting" I simply mean being totally with what is here. Not moving away or toward something else, just remaining with the whole thing—an intense presence that includes all the bodily sensations, breathing, wind-storming, raining, sunning, birding, coughing, fans humming—everything right here, all at once, without a seam. Observing thoughts coming up, emotions about to be triggered, physical sensations arising and more thoughts, emotions, feelings, sensations unfolding and abating—being with it all. There isn't any place to escape to. Everything is here without separation.

Let thoughts come up, let them reveal themselves for what they are and disappear. It all is the stuff of dreams, traces from the infinite past. Thoughts may trigger fear, but fear too can become transparency. When it arises, here it is. Let it be. Don't call it by name—labels attract memories and reactions from the past. No need to have any feelings about it—they too are empty. Fear is an unavoidable occurrence in our habitual self-centered consciousness. We cannot possibly live the illusion of a separate *me* without experiencing fears about what may happen to it. But illusions and dreams can also be seen as just dreams and illusions, even though they can arouse tremendous inner turbulence in the form of horror, agony, or pleasure. It is all part and parcel of human consciousness manifesting as separate *me* and *you.*

Sitting quietly, watching things come up time and time again, a tape may be playing: "Is *that* what meditation is all about? I don't want to spend the rest of my meditative life watching endless repetitions of garbage." But the important thing is not *what* is seen but the quality of the seeing. When a person asks, "Is watching the comings and goings of thoughts and emotions all there is to meditation?" I say that it all depends on the quality of the watching. Is it consumed by judging, by feeling guilty, ashamed, or impatient? As those mental movements occur, see them for what they are and don't be disturbed by them. That is choiceless awareness—no separate watcher occupying center stage. The inner show is simply displaying itself on its own and needs no particular audience, no applause or rejection. Let it all happen as it is happening in the infinite space of open presence.

Is "choiceless awareness" just another dream, a new illusion? Thought can turn anything into a concept by thinking and dreaming about it. See it when it happens and don't be fooled by it. Choiceless awareness is not an illusion. It is here for human beings like you and me. Transparency unfolds on its own, revealing all there is as it is, in utter directness and simplicity, without need for a director.

Actually, awareness is here even during times of darkness. Presence never goes anywhere. This is not a dogmatic statement but a simple fact that each one of us can come upon. See the cloud, the darkness! Hear the wind! Feel the breathing! Smell the flowers! Touch the swaying grasses! Clouds, wind, thoughts, breathing, fragrant flowers, and grasses change all the time, but seeing is here without time. Even though doubts may obscure it, it is here the instant the mind stops and every cell of the body opens up to hear and see and be.

No need to bother one's head about what has been said. Being present is all of oneself, not just the head! We are this entire living creation from moment to moment without a break. Walk innocently through the fields, into the woods, along the ocean beach or in the city streets with the sheer joy of aliveness, its infinite movements and sounds and fragrance—the love of it all without making a thing out of it!

Are we here?

28

Tracking the Two Bodies

A CONVERSATION BETWEEN TONI PACKER AND LENORE FRIEDMAN

*T*ONI AND LENORE are sitting in front of the fire in Lenore's living room two days before Toni's annual retreat in California. It is the end of a rainy afternoon in late December. People will be arriving for dinner in a couple of hours, but right now there is time to continue a conversation started a year before, in which Toni had mentioned "two bodies—the conditioned and the unconditioned." This year Toni is not so sure about these terms and suggests we look at them freshly, to see if they are a good description or not.

LENORE FRIEDMAN: What I understood last year was that the conditioned body is the one that corresponds to all our ideas and thoughts about ourselves, our expectations, our re-

Originally published in slightly different form in *Being Bodies* by Lenore Friedman and Susan Moon (Boston: Shambhala Publications, Inc., 1997).

sistance, all the repetitive stuff that goes on because of past conditioning and present conditioning. Which we keep re-peating and re-creating.

TONI PACKER: It keeps repeating and re-creating itself. Yes.

LF: In this conditioned body there is rigidity, holding, contraction . . .

TP: Patterning. Yes.

LF: As contrasted to the unconditioned state, which would be fluid, open—open to change, to the present moment.

TP: Open in awareness.

LF: Where does awareness reside?

TP: I don't know. I don't know where it resides, but it isn't separate from the body either. It permeates and contains everything and yet it is beyond everything. Language is prob-lematic, the thing itself is very clear. It is the clarity, the wholeness of it all. And the sharpness of the senses, function-ing as one whole perception.

LF: Let's go back to two bodies . . .

TP: Two bodies, a conditioned and an unconditioned, or a new and an old body I've sometimes called it.

LF: A new body . . . a place you arrive, as opposed to a place you've been?

TP: No. It's not something you have achieved. It is the real home, one's true being. The other is distorted, blocked func-tioning, self-enclosing thoughts and emotions.

LF: So these days do you prefer the terms the new and old body?

TP: No . . . these days I don't hang on to words. None of them are as good as seeing, experiencing directly what is actually happening.

LF: We should just quit talking now! (*laughs*) Still, I want to ask if we're talking about actual structures—organs, muscles, bone—or are we merely talking about processes? I mean, is there a difference in the way that the structures function in the two bodies?

TP: I'm quite sure that there is.

LF: How would you describe that?

TP: You mean is there a difference in how the physical structures are functioning when there is presence right now? When there is clear awareness? If I stay completely with what is observed at this very moment, habitual tensions become transparent and smooth out.

LF: Yes, in fact that just happened to me! I first noticed a thought, and it had to do with the time. There's something I have to do in about twenty minutes, to prepare for dinner, and in my belly I could feel this tightening. When I noticed it, it relented.

TP: If it hadn't been detected it would have continued. But let's look further. Does a physical tension of stress, hurriedness, "I have no time"—the kind of physical tension that goes with those thoughts—does it keep on going without supporting thoughts?

LF: Perhaps habitual tensions *create* thoughts.

TP: Yes, because a physical tension creates the thought, "There must be something to worry about!"

LF: And we're up in our heads again—with tension in our shoulders and our necks, we're thinking, figuring things out, problem solving. It's self-defensive and self-preservatory and it has a kind of "up-thereness" to it. Which I guess would correspond to the conditioned body. Whereas residing in the lower body seems to allow things to slow down.

TP: There's a danger here, though, that I went through in Zen training, where we were deliberately trying, forcing, to put our energy into our lower belly. I called it the "elevator effect": first the intention from the head to let the energy go down, then some sensation in the belly, then wondering up in the head how I'm doing. Up and down, down and up. And yet there is definitely something to this energy gathering low in the body that allows the head to be light, free, open, unencumbered. And therefore naturally intelligent.

LF: Could you amplify this?

TP: Entering into silence, sitting quietly, allowing whatever is happening "inside" and "out" to reveal itself freely, meditatively, brings about a natural shift of energy from head, neck, and shoulders, to the foundation of this bodymind—an enlivening of the entire organism.

LF: Would you say that the new body or the unconditioned body would be one where there isn't this kind of split (top from bottom) in the body? Is that what's intelligent? That there's a feedback loop, a conversation or collaboration going on?

TP: Yes.

LF: I know that awareness is not just inside our skins. The organism is fully awake and perceiving reality and responding to it. Resting in it, part of a vaster awareness.

TP: It *is* reality. One wholeness of functioning.

LF: Toni, would you articulate the two-bodies idea in a way that really feels accurate to you?

TP: Can we say that the new body is no separate body? Nobody? It is the best I can come up with. You said you know it is not just within our skin, but is there even a skin?

LF: Not without holes.

TP: The more powerful the microscope or telescope, the more empty space reveals itself. That is not just an item of physics that we can know, but something very palpable.

LF: When the energy is high up, in the head, then there is absolute conviction that the skin is not only solid and separating us, but that it also requires defense.

TP: Yes. And when the energy knots up high in the head, entangled in thoughts and images and proclamations imagined to be real, the whole body becomes mobilized or immobilized with emotionality. It cannot perceive that it is an integral part of everything else that's going on around it. It feels encapsulated, enclosed, isolated. Thought has an uncanny ability to trigger physical processes that originally were not meant to react to thought. They evolved to react to real dangers or needs.

LF: Can you say some more about this?

TP: When a deer in the meadow sees you approaching, it instantly stops grazing and looks at you motionlessly. The white tail, used to signal danger to other deer, twitches slightly now and then, ready to flash at any time. If you come too close or move abruptly, up goes the tail like a torch and the animals bound gracefully into the woods for cover. For us humans no presence of genuine physical danger is needed for the whole body to be flooded by waves of anxiety. All it takes is one scary thought, one fearful memory, one threatening image to trigger physical flight or fight or freeze reactions. Imagining we are alone and isolated, abandoned, causes immediate pain and sorrow. Deer most likely don't ruminate about being separate creatures—it spares them a lifetime of mental grief!

It is clear that the body itself learns something about this amazing being-in-awareness. At Springwater, I usually go to our beautiful sitting hall in the morning, and in the freedom of sitting quietly, the seamless depth of it, the body is learning the organismic way of open being. It becomes natural. Awareness is here on its own. When any effort is made—the intention to be aware—there isn't this ease of just being here. That is the beauty of it: when there is the ease of simple being, which means no blockages, no enclosures, no separation, there is not even the possibility of making an effort. In the state that we've been calling the "new body," there is no need for effort because the barking dog "outside" is right here, it is not separate. There is no effort "to be one with it" as we used to say in Zen. We are already one whole movement in sound and silence.

LF: There's no need to get from here to there.

TP: No need to get from here to there because *there* is already *here!* This just needs to dawn fully! The aware body does not feel that anything is outside of it. Nothing is separate.

LF: As we've been talking, at moments that's felt quite palpable.

TP: Yes, just sitting here and talking together, feeling the inwardness, intensity, and depth, there is immense energy—

not so much a physical body feeling, but palpitating, vibrating energy.

LF: A very alive energy . . . with no sense of where I begin or end particularly, just that alive moment.

TP: The intelligence of awareness leaves that whole network of self-reference, I-centeredness alone—it needn't be entered. All the energy gathers here right now. Body is energy. In the presence of this aware listening—voices, breathing, noises—there is no need for energy to travel into the "me" network. (Once the me-network is mobilized through inattention, the body contracts into its old habitual patterns.)

About twenty years ago, sitting in a zendo, trying to be a good meditator way into the night, I noticed clearly for the first time how every once in a while in the midst of quiet, unconcerned sitting, the brain would click in with the question: "Am I doing all right?" "Am I getting somewhere?" When the "am I doing it right?" tape became transparent, it was also clear that I don't have to know how I am doing! Sitting quietly is *not knowing*. But first you have to clearly recognize the tremendous desire to know. Not just thinking about it, but experiencing it directly as it is happening. This is how we're built, how we've evolved. It's wonderful to see this powerful urge to know, to question it, and to realize that maybe I don't have to know everything. Not knowing, the body is at ease. Not knowing doesn't mean not hearing the words. The words arise but the brain isn't concerned.

LF: In that state, it almost feels pointless to talk.

TP: Yes!

LF: As I sit here and settle, following your words, letting go of self-preoccupation, the impulse, the fuel behind my questions seems to subside. The charge has gone out of them.

TP: What is the charge behind the question?

LF: A couple of paradoxical things sort of gnaw at me and also excite me. But if I'm just being, the energy drains away.

TP: Let's articulate the paradoxes, because the brain wants to make order, wants to finish its business and does not want to carry a lot of unresolved things around. It wants to resolve conflict. What are the paradoxes?

LF: Well, there are times, usually when I'm sitting, that I experience a kind of quietness in which there isn't any edge to me. The body exists and doesn't exist. It's filled with open spaces and holes, breath and energy moving in and out, or back and forth. The idea of inside and outside seems arbitrary. So one paradox I guess is the body and the no-body, both present in a sort of embodiedness that rests in a larger, undiscriminated whole.

TP: Does it rest in it or is it that large, undiscriminated whole? Where does the arm end and the fingers begin? Where do the fingers end and space begins?

LF: There—I started thinking again and I moved right back to self-concern!

TP: So thinking creates the conditioned body. We know how certain ways of thinking either twist our faces and bodies or relax them. Our faces express our past and present thoughts and feelings, fears and desires. Our bodies grow and relax or contort according to how we think about ourselves and how others think about us. We embody what our parents thought about us. I see so many subtle changes in children growing up, the way they walk, the way the eyes look, the way the mouth and shoulders are held. Yet it is simple to let openness permeate this physical structure and let it dissolve.

LF: The physical structure dissolves?

TP: The idea about it does. Without the idea about my body, it all feels quite different, more natural.

LF: Is there time for one more paradox? We've been talking about the openness of the body, but there is also the defensive structure of the body. This body that seems so obviously to be us—there's me and you and them, all in our separate bodies, and then all the defensive operations come into play from perceiving "them" as separate.

TP: The body hardens, stiffens, mobilizes for defense or aggression.

LF: Yes. Because the separate you can threaten the separate me.

TP: Instinctive protective impulses stay alive because the organism loves to live—life loves to stay alive and propagate itself.

LF: Love? Can we talk about love, and how it is of the body and *not* of the body?

TP: Love is intrinsic to the openness of being. The enclosed, imprisoned, is not loving, it can't love, it is choking.

LF: But when you say the body loves to live . . . is that another kind of love?

TP: Love is to live, love is to continue. Life loves to live, loves to continue and propagate itself, to create ever new forms. Are you asking, how does that relate to the love that naturally lights up the human heart when self-concern is quiet? Do we need to first differentiate, and then relate again what the mind has separated, or can we behold it all in silent wonderment?

29

Listening to It All

WHAT A BEAUTIFUL, crisp morning it is, inviting to enter. Walking up the fire trail behind the retreat center, one finds an amazing harmony of light and shade, coolness and warmth, the roar of distant traffic and the tranquillity of the eucalyptus grove. Continuing up the shady trail and suddenly entering into bright sunlight—wonder of wonders: a new bench has appeared right on the edge of the path where the hill slopes down toward the bay. The bench is sturdily grounded as though it could outlast the next millennium! Sitting comfortably on the smooth boards, one faces the densely populated hills across the valley and, way down below, the sparkling streams of tiny cars and trucks flowing back and forth along narrow white bands. Bustling canyons in the valley, and above everything the vast blue sky stretching out with not a cloud in sight. As one climbs farther along the trail, winding through dry hills away from houses, people, and cars, there is just green chaparral on each side of the path with sandy stones crunching underfoot. No destination in sight or mind.

The question arises frequently: Is there any relationship between our turbulent daily life out in the world and the

quiet sitting here at retreat, any relationship between our restless busyness and the peaceful leisure of retreating, between
stress and repose, between overcrowded space and simple
openness?

Do we want to find out? Let's walk up to that bench on
the edge of the trail and sit down between heaven and earth,
beholding the wondrous harmony of light and shade, rush
and rest, noise and tranquillity, space and crowdedness without any movement of thought bringing preferences into the
picture. No need to think about oneself—the picture is already complete: everything is here, with all the seemingly ir-
reconcilable opposites vibrantly alive this moment, flowing
harmoniously out of this one silent, grounded bench.

It's a bench of fresh looking and listening. Not our old,
conventional ways that are automatic, conditioned, repetitive,
and disturbed by judgments, wanting people and things to
be different, afraid to be worse, needing to know, craving to
continue. Usually we perceive everything through an opaque
film of attitudes and stories. Can they be irradiated with attention so that the dense filter becomes luminously transparent? As long as we don't actively notice the opinions and
beliefs filtering our perceptions, our listening is not clear and
accurate. It is caught up and distorted—not in touch with
what is actually here from moment to moment—simple, unadorned presence without any lack.

Open listening embraces all the senses as one whole perception. There is no division between looking, listening,
smelling, touching, or tasting—just undivided openness of
all senses perceiving as one whole without a separate *me* at
work. There is no doer and no recipient here—just spontaneous presence without fragmentation.

Can we begin to listen freshly to all the internal noise?
By internal noise I mean the inner monologuing, dialoguing,

arguing, contradicting, wanting, obsessing, angering, guilt-ing—whatever may be going on this instant. Not listening in order to judge or get rid of what arises, but beginning to notice inwardly what is happening here right now in silent wonderment.

Somebody asked earlier about dropping the self. There is no such thing as someone dropping the self. Who would be dropping what? What we have believed to be an independent *me* residing somewhere within this bodymind and controlling things turns out to be an intricate network of discrete memo-ries, ideas, impulses, and reactions moving together with sen-sations and emotions. This whole movement either comes into awareness, maybe just faintly, partially in the beginning, or else it is misinterpreted or ignored. See what happens when the inner commotion begins to reveal itself! What hap-pens to a reaction like jealousy as it comes into awareness? Does it continue unabatedly because it is so powerful, so primal? Or can the inexhaustible energy of wondering, of seeing and understanding intelligently begin to replace a ha-bitual reaction?

Can awareness take the place of an agitating story line that is thoroughly seen through and understood?

This morning has never been here before. Never. And it will not be here again. That's why it's so fresh, so new, so full of vitality and beauty as it resounds with the roar of traffic winding through narrow canyons and, at the same time, permeated with light and air and sky.

As we listen inwardly to our pains and joys, feeling the body tensing and relaxing, the heart beating faster and slower, the breath flowing rapidly and calmly—can we behold it all in innocent wonderment? Thoughts, stories, emotions, and judgments are swirling around in empty space like dust parti-cles visible in a beam of light. Emptiness is not a mysterious concept. It is the absence of needing to be *me* to interfere, to control. It is the absence of resistance. Have you ever felt absence of resistance? Unconditionally yielding to what is? The traffic sign "yield" says: "Don't forge ahead but watch carefully because cars are coming dangerously fast. Let them pass! Look and listen! There will be an opening to merge with the traffic."

In our bustling daily life we may feel that we have neither the time nor place to listen quietly, to look freshly. But if we are truly interested in a place and time to listen, an opportunity will present itself. It is one of the amazing graces of being alive that when there is a small flame of yearning to find out, we unexpectedly come upon a bench to sit on out in the open and realize that there is more space in this universe than the tight cocoon we have lived in all our life.

With renewed questioning comes new wondering and listening. Heaven and earth are open in simply being here as we are, breathing in and out with an airplane humming in the sky—the miracle of this moment! Nothing is separate. Everything is here as it is, utterly simple. No one is here to lay any claim to it.